W9-AGG-680

IN DEFENSE OF THE DECALOGUE

A CRITIQUE OF NEW COVENANT THEOLOGY

"...I WILL PUT MY LAW IN
THEIR MINDS, AND WRITE IT
ON THEIR HEARTS..."
—JEREMIAH 31:33

"DO NOT THINK THAT I CAME
TO DESTROY THE LAW OR THE
PROPHETS, I DID NOT COME
TO DESTROY BUT TO FULFILL."
—MATTHEW 5:17

"DO WE THEN MAKE VOID THE
LAW THROUGH FAITH? GOD
FORBID; YEA, WE ESTABLISH
THE LAW."
—ROMANS 3:31

RICHARD C. BARCELLOS

WINEPRESS WP PUBLISHING

© 2001 by Richard Barcellos. All rights reserved.

Printed in the United States of America.

Packaged by WinePress Publishing, PO Box 428, Enumclaw, WA 98022. The views expressed or implied in this work do not necessarily reflect those of WinePress Publishing. Ultimate design, content, and editorial accuracy of this work is the responsibility of the author.

No part of this publication may be reproduced, stored in a retrieval system or transmitted in any way by any means, electronic, mechanical, photocopy, recording or otherwise, without the prior permission of the copyright holder except as provided by USA copyright law.

Unless otherwise noted all scriptures are taken from the New King James Version, Copyright © 1979, 1980, 1982 by Thomas Nelson, Inc., Publishers. Used by permission.

ISBN 0-9654955-9-0
Library of Congress Catalog Card Number: 00-109481

Richard Barcellos has made a significant contribution to current debate among Calvinistic Baptists concerning the law of God. It is clearly argued, biblically anchored and historically aware. While his case is presented forcefully, his spirit remains charitable. Everyone who recognizes the importance of the relationship which God has established between His law and His gospel should carefully read this book.

Thomas K. Ascol, Ph.D.
Pastor, Grace Baptist Church, Cape Coral, FL
Editor, Founders Journal, FL

••

A mantra has gripped the evangelical world that says that we who live in the New Testament age do not have to obey the Old Testament moral law found in the Ten Words, or a similar statement in other words. Pastor Barcellos has taken very seriously one manifestation of that view and has shown how clearly it fails to follow the teaching of the Scriptures themselves on this very question. If you want to know whether God intends for you as a New Testament Christian to obey his Ten Commandments by all means get this work and compare its perspective to the Scriptures themselves.

George W. Knight, III, Th.D.
Adjunct Professor, Greenville Presbyterian Theological Seminary, SC

••

Pastor Richard Barcellos' book In Defense of the Decalogue provides the Church with a much-needed corrective to the misguided views promoted in our day under the general title New Covenant Theology. With an irenic spirit, he examines many of the key writings of the advocates of this system and identifies exegetical, theological and historical problems contained in them. He skillfully demonstrates the weaknesses in these views, and works hard to establish a Scriptural basis for the Reformed confessional position.

At root, his work is exegetical. He seeks to engage the text of Scripture carefully, handling grammatical, contextual and linguistic matters in some detail. Exegesis leads to theological reasoning, and Pastor Barcellos shows much ability in the integration of the various facets of doctrine involved in this study.

It is a significant contribution to the contemporary debate.

James M. Renihan, Ph.D.
Dean, Institute of Reformed Baptist Studies
Westminster Theological Seminary, CA
••

Rev. Barcellos' book In Defense of the Decalogue: A Critique of New Covenant Theology clearly presents the case of historical and confessional covenantal theology over against this new teaching which is nothing more than implicit dispensationalism. Rev. Barcellos has brilliantly identified the unbiblical errors upon which this man-made doctrine has been established. This book is sound theological treatment in defense of biblical covenantal thought. I recommend this book to everyone who is interested in preserving the truth of God's covenantal promises as revealed in the Holy Scriptures.

Kenneth G. Talbot, Ph.D., Th.D.
President, Whitefield Theological Seminary, FL
••

There is no greater danger to historic, Reformed Christianity today than the assault on its emphasis on the law of God. The moral law of God, as epitomized in the Ten Commandments according to Reformed and Puritan Christianity, binds all men everywhere until Christ returns. The rampant antinomian attack on this great doctrine threatens the very foundations of biblical Christianity. The Christian community owes, therefore, a debt to Pastor Barcellos' book, In Defense of the Decalogue. This book mounts a devastating counterattack on one of the most subtle and dangerous attacks on the Reformed doctrine of the law of God.

Samuel E. Waldron, Th.M.
Pastor, The Reformed Baptist Church of Grand Rapids, Grand Rapids, MI
Principal, Reformed Baptist School of Theology, MI
••

The relation of the Old and New Testaments is a complex issue which has long puzzled Christian interpreters, and it is a perennial issue which has loomed large among Calvinistic Baptists in our own day. In addressing some of us on "the other side," our friend Richard Barcellos has taken a much-needed step in the advancement of this discussion. His exegetical outlook is commendable, and he has addressed some issues which well-deserve further attention. I am sure this will provide a catalyst for a good deal of discussion in the months ahead.

Fred G. Zaspel, Th.M.
Pastor, Word of Life Baptist Church, Pottsville, PA
Adjunct Professor of Religious Studies, Penn State University, PA
••••••••••••••••••••••••••••••••••

Preface

Issues of continuity and discontinuity between the Testaments are some of the most difficult to grasp in all of theology. For many years, Covenant theologians and Dispensational theologians have locked horns on these issues, producing many books, articles, and debates on the subject. One recent entrant into the debate has been New Covenant Theology. This theology seeks to strike a middle ground between the stress on continuity in traditional Reformed theology and the radical discontinuity of some older forms of Dispensationalism. Yet the question that must be asked is: Is it biblical? Does New Covenant Theology accurately reflect the teaching of the Bible? It is this author's contention that some of the major tenets of New Covenant Theology are not biblical and do not accurately reflect the teaching of the Bible. I also believe New Covenant Theology is troublesome because it produces a reductionistic, myopic and truncated view of Christian ethics. This book offers a biblical critique of New Covenant Theology.

The critique in no way pretends to be exhaustive. It reflects my own limited, and certainly fallible, understanding of New Covenant Theology. Frankly, it is somewhat difficult to critique New Covenant Theology for at least three reasons. First, New Covenant Theology is not a monolithic movement. New Covenant theologians differ on some of the nuances involved with defining New Covenant Theology. Second, New Covenant Theology is a relatively new school of thought. Though there is much in print on New Covenant Theology, there is no definitive work as yet. Third, one major adherent of New Covenant Theology has recently acknowledged that he will have to modify his understanding of the Old Covenant and revise some of his published works. Because of these things, a critique can become quickly outdated.

I have based my critique upon what is in print and thus fully realize that it may need to be modified in the days to come. However, I have attempted to examine some of the major tenets of New Covenant Theology (which New Covenant theologians appear to express basic agreement upon) without which New Covenant Theology ceases to exist. I not only critique these major tenets but also offer exegetically based answers to the issues at stake. Therefore, the critique ends up being a defense of the perpetuity of the Decalogue as well. This is why I have entitled the book *In Defense of the Decalogue*.

This critique is aimed at pastors and theological students, though it is hoped that any studious Christian will profit from its contents. Those not interested in technical, secondary points may skip the footnotes. However, the reader should know that the footnotes also contain some crucial justifications for arguments made in the main text, for those inclined to delve deeper.

I want to express my deep appreciation to Founders Press for expressing interest in this work. Special thanks go to Dr. Tom Ascol and Mr. Ernest Reisinger for their encouragement and support. Thanks also to Dr. George W. Knight, III, Dr. James M. Renihan, Dr. Kenneth G. Talbot, and Pastors Earl M. Blackburn, Albert N. Martin, Samuel E. Waldron, and Fred G. Zaspel for reading the manuscript and offering help along the way.

May the Lord continue to bless the labors of Founders Press and bring about a theological and practical reformation, not only in the Southern Baptist Convention, but also throughout the world and in all of the Lord's true churches.

Soli Deo gloria!

Richard C. Barcellos
September 2000

Table of Contents

Introduction

New Covenant Theology is a movement within conservative, Evangelical, and Calvinistic Baptist circles, which seeks to steer a middle road between traditional Covenant Theology and Dispensational Theology. The movement arose, in part, due to a concern with traditional Covenant Theology's emphasis on continuity and a concern with Dispensational Theology's emphasis on discontinuity between the Old and New Covenants. The position ends up modifying both traditional Covenant Theology and traditional Dispensational Theology in the areas of ecclesiology (Israel/Church) and ethics (law/grace).

New Covenant Theology attempts to base its conclusions on the exegesis of key texts that speak to the issues of continuity and discontinuity in both the Old and New Testaments. One key Old Testament text for New Covenant Theology is found in Jeremiah 31:31–34. According to New Covenant Theology, this text teaches us that the Old Covenant will be abrogated and replaced by the New Covenant. New Covenant theologians hold that Jeremiah 31 leaves us with the expectation that along with a New Covenant comes a new law, which is a higher and more spiritual law than the Law of Moses. They believe this new, more spiritual law is called the law of Christ and is mentioned in 1 Corinthians 9:21 and, especially, Galatians 6:2.

According to New Covenant Theology, this perspective on New Covenant law is supported by Christ's use of the Mosaic Law in the Sermon on the Mount as recorded in Matthew 5–7.[1] Christ is seen as the new lawgiver of the New Covenant based on the promise of Deuteronomy 18. His new law incorporates selective

---

1. See John Reisinger, *But I Say Unto You*, (Southbridge, MA: Crown Publications, Inc., 1989).

aspects of the Law of Moses, but not its whole. New Covenant theologians also hold that Jeremiah 31 leaves us with the expectation that the New Covenant community will be comprised of believers only (those who know the Lord). They contend this is supported by many New Testament texts, such as Galatians 3:7, 9, 26–29, and the fact that baptism, the Lord's Supper, and other New Covenant privileges are reserved for believers.

One key New Testament text for New Covenant Theology is found in Matthew 5:17–20. According to New Covenant Theology, this text teaches that though law as embodied in the Old Testament is not totally done away with under the New Covenant, it does undergo a redemptive-historical shift in application.[2] For instance, New Covenant Theology teaches that the Sabbath, under the New Covenant, refers to our soteriological rest in Christ, not the Lord's Day.

Another key New Testament text for New Covenant Theology is Ephesians 2:14–15. According to New Covenant Theology, this text teaches that the Law of Moses was destroyed by the death of Christ, thus making ethics dependent upon Christ, not Moses. In addition, New Covenant theologians believe this text teaches that the Church is a new work of God and not merely a continuation of Old Covenant Israel.[3]

There are many facets of New Covenant Theology that all ought to appreciate. Every Christian should appreciate its high view of Scripture; its respect for the sovereignty of God in salvation and providence; its attempts to understand the nature of, and relationship between, the various biblical covenants; its attempts to wrestle with the issues related to continuity and discontinuity between the Testaments; its insistence that we ground theology in exegesis; and finally, its attempts to understand the redemptive-historical effects of Christ's death and its

---

2. Fred G. Zaspel, "Divine Law: A New Covenant Perspective," *Reformation & Revival, Volume 6, Number 3,* (Carol Stream, IL: Reformation & Revival Ministries, Inc., Summer 1997), 145–169.

3. See Carl B. Hoch, Jr. *All Things New,* (Grand Rapids, MI: Baker Books, 1995), 172–178 for a view of the relationship between Israel and the Church, based on Ephesians 2:15, which is sympathetic to New Covenant Theology. In the mind of at least one prominent New Covenant theologian, Hoch's book is

implications for New Testament theology. New Covenant Theology has produced some challenging exegetical critiques of both traditional Covenant Theology and Dispensational Theology. New Covenant Theology seeks to call all Christians to sound exegesis and biblical theology. New Covenant theologians are zealous students of the Bible and are attempting to submit themselves to its teaching. For these and other things, New Covenant Theology is to be applauded.

At the same time, however, there are some issues related to New Covenant Theology that should disturb us and are worth challenging. This critique focuses on New Covenant Theology and ethics. It critiques New Covenant Theology in the following eight areas: (1) New Covenant Theology's view of the promise of the New Covenant; (2) New Covenant Theology's view concerning the identity of the Old Covenant; (3) New Covenant Theology's views related to the abolition of the Old Covenant; (4) New Covenant Theology's perspective on the Sermon on the Mount; (5) New Covenant Theology's position on the identity of the Moral Law; (6) New Covenant Theology's hermeneutical presuppositions; (7) New Covenant Theology implications for canonics; and finally, (8) New Covenant Theology and historical theology. In evaluating each of these topics, the general method of approach will be to first identify the specific issue at hand and the New Covenant Theology position on that topic, then to provide a biblical critique of the New Covenant Theology position, and next to summarize the exegetical challenge presented to New Covenant Theology from the biblical text. After reviewing each of these topics, some brief conclusions will be drawn and pertinent challenges presented to New Covenant Theology.

As shown in the pages that follow, this critique ends up being a defense of the perpetuity of the Decalogue, hence the title.

"[b]y far and away . . . at the top of the list for resources on the new covenant." See John H. Armstrong, "Annotated Bibliography," *Reformation & Revival, Volume 6, Number 3,* 195.

New Covenant Theology and the Promise of the New Covenant

The Issue at Stake

The first area of challenge for New Covenant Theology concerns its central thesis, that the law written on the heart in the New Covenant is decidedly not the same as the law of the Mosaic Covenant. The issue under consideration is what Jeremiah meant when he said in Jeremiah 31:31–34 that "I will put *My law* in their minds, and write it on their hearts" (emphasis added). This is a key text; in fact, it is the only text in the Old Testament that mentions the New Covenant by name. This makes it the beginning point in a study of New Covenant Theology.

In a *Reformation & Revival Journal* on the New Covenant, New Covenant theologian Geoff Adams seems to identify the law written on the heart as prophesied by Jeremiah as the Decalogue.[1] However, in *Tablets of Stone*, in a chapter entitled "The Ten Commandments Were Given Only To the Nation of Israel," John Reisinger says, ". . . the Ten Commandments, as the covenant [Old Covenant] document, was given only to the nation Israel. . . ."[2] Reisinger goes on to attempt to prove that this means the Decalogue cannot function *as a unit* under the New Covenant. Reisinger's position appears to be the standard

---

1. Geoff Adams, "The New Covenant of Jeremiah 31:31–37," *Reformation & Revival, Volume 6, Number 3,* 83–85.

2. John Reisinger, *Tablets of Stone,* (Southbridge, MA: Crown Publications, Inc., 1989), 43.

New Covenant Theology position. Most New Covenant theologians would *not* identify the law written on the heart in Jeremiah 31:33 as the Decalogue.

EXPOSITION OF JEREMIAH 31:33

A careful exegesis of Jeremiah 31:31–34, however, severely undercuts the New Covenant Theology position in this regard. Commenting on this passage, Walter C. Kaiser, Jr. says:

> This is the only place in the OT where the expression "new covenant" (31:31) occurs; however, it would appear that the concept was much more widespread. . . . Still, Jeremiah 31:31–34 was the *locus classicus* on the subject, as may be seen from several lines of evidence. . . . it was also the largest piece of text to be quoted *in extenso* in the NT, viz., Hebrews 8:8–12, and partially repeated a few chapters later in Hebrews 10:16–17. Furthermore, it was the subject of nine other NT texts: four dealing with the Lord's Supper (Matt. 26:28; Mark 14:24; Luke 22:20; 1 Cor. 11:25); two Pauline references to "ministers of the new covenant" and the future forgiveness of Israel's sins (2 Cor. 3:6; Rom. 11:27); and three additional references in Hebrews (9:15; 10:16; 12:24; cf. the two large teaching passages mentioned above).[3]

Quite obviously, then, when considering the New Covenant from the Old Testament, the place to start is Jeremiah 31:31–34. Due to the focus of our subject, we will concentrate on the law written on the heart as promised in verse 33.

The text of Jeremiah 31:33 reads:

> But this *is* the covenant that I will make with the house of Israel after those days, says the LORD: I will put My law in their minds, and write it on their hearts; and I will be their God, and they shall be My people.

A few observations will serve our purpose. First, notice that the law under the New Covenant is God's law, something that He

---

3. Walter C. Kaiser, Jr., *Toward an Old Testament Theology*, (Grand Rapids, MI: Zondervan Publishing House, 1978, re. 1991), 231–232.

both authors and possesses. In verse 33, we read, "I will put *My law* [emphasis added] in their minds, and write *it* [emphasis added] on their hearts." *My law* and *it* refer to the same thing. The phrase "My law" occurs six times in the book of Jeremiah (Jer. 6:19, 9:13, 16:11, 26:4, 31:33, and 44:10). In these contexts, "My law" is described as something that can be heard; something that was set before the Old Covenant people of God; something that is equated with God's voice; something that can be not kept; something that when not kept is considered as forsaking God and committing idolatry; something that can be listened to; something that can be transgressed; something that will be written on the heart; and something that was set before the fathers. It is very clear that Jeremiah is referring to an objective standard of known and expected conduct when he uses the phrase "My law." Whatever this law is, we know that it is not our law but God's law already revealed to God's Old Covenant people.

Second, notice that the law of God under the New Covenant will be put on the mind, written on the heart of all the beneficiaries of the New Covenant. This promised blessing of the New Covenant of the law written on the heart is to be enjoyed by the whole New Covenant community. The law of God written on the heart will be universal within that community, just as the saving knowledge of God and the forgiveness of sins (see verse 34). In other words, the New Covenant community is a saved, regenerate community.

Third, notice that God is both the author of the law itself and the one who writes it on the heart. In effect, God says, "I will put and write My law on the minds and hearts of My New Covenant people."

These observations provide the exegetical groundwork necessary for identifying the basic, fundamental law of God under the New Covenant referred to by Jeremiah. The text of Jeremiah clearly assumes that the law of God under the New Covenant is referring to a law that was already written at the time of the writing of Jeremiah. The phrase "My law," when referring to God, always refers to something revealed by Him to Israel, not

only in the book of Jeremiah, but in the whole Old Testament.[4]
The language of God Himself *writing* a law is familiar Old Testa-
ment language. This is illustrated in Exodus 31:18, which says,
"And when He had made an end of speaking with him on Mount
Sinai, He gave Moses two tablets of the Testimony, tablets of
stone, *written* [emphasis added] with the finger of God." Exodus 31:18 must have entered the minds of Jeremiah's audience,
steeped in Old Testament language and theology as they were.[5]
Jeremiah clearly teaches that the law of God under the New
Covenant is a law that both *has been* and *will be* written by God
Himself. If we allow antecedent Old Testament theology to inform the writer, the original audience, and all subsequent hear-
ers, the only plausible answer to the question concerning the
identity of the law is that it must be the same law God Himself
wrote previously. This is the natural assumption of the text.

Understood this way, Jeremiah clearly teaches that the law
of God under the New Covenant is a law that *was* written on
stone by God and that *will be* written on hearts by God. Exodus
24:12 identifies the "tablets of stone" with "the law and commandments which I have written." This is a very important verse,
for it uses the Hebrew word *torah* [law] as a synonym for what
God wrote on stones. In the *New International Dictionary of Old
Testament Theology and Exegesis*, Peter Enns acknowledges that
torah [law] refers to the Decalogue in this text, when he says,

---

4. See Exodus 16:4; 2 Chronicles 6:16; Psalm 89:30; Isaiah 51:7; Jeremiah 6:19, 9:13, 16:11, 26:4, 31:33, 44:10; Ezekiel 22:26; and Hosea 8:1, 12.
The phrase is also used in contexts not referring to God in Psalm 78:1; Proverbs 3:1, 4:2; and 7:2.

5. I realize that the prophecy looks forward in redemptive history, which
might cause some to conclude that we must wait for subsequent revelation to
define the law of the New Covenant for us. I agree with this, in part. For
instance, Hebrews 8:10 says, ". . . I will put *My laws* [emphasis added] in
their mind and write *them* [emphasis added] on their hearts. . . ." This text in
no way negates the exposition of Jeremiah 31:33 as referring to the Decalogue. It simply argues for a redemptive-historical expansion and application
of Jeremiah's prophecy. In other words, as with other uses of the Old Testament by the New, the fulfillment of Jeremiah 31:33 illustrates the principle of
sensus plenior (Old Testament texts contain a *fuller sense* than intended by the

"Other uses of *torah* [law] include: a reference to the stone tablets (Exod. 24:12). . . ."[6]

Let us compare Exodus 31:18, Jeremiah 31:33, and 2 Corinthians 3:3. Here are these texts in canonical order: "And when He had made an end of speaking with him on Mount Sinai, He gave Moses two tablets of the Testimony, tablets of stone, written with the finger of God." "But this *is the* covenant that I will make with the house of Israel after those days, says the LORD: I will put My law in their minds, and write it on their hearts; and I will be their God, and they shall be My people." "[C]learly you are an epistle of Christ, ministered by us, written not with ink but by the Spirit of the living God, not on tablets of stone but on tablets of flesh, *that is,* of the heart." Thus, both antecedent revelation (Exod. 31:18) and subsequent revelation (2 Cor. 3:3) force us to reckon with the fact that the law of God, written by God Himself, was what He wrote on stone.[7] In a very unique way, the Ten Commandments comprise *the* law of God. All other Old Covenant laws were both mediated through Moses and written by Moses.[8] The Ten Commandments were first written by God and then written by Moses. We conclude the terms of the

---

author, which awaits further revelation from God for its meaning.). It will be argued below that the understanding of the law being referred to by Jeremiah as the Ten Commandments is not only supported by the Old Testament, but by the New as well. In other words, what the Old Testament promises, the New Testament fulfills.

6. Willem A. Van Gemeren, General Editor, *New International Dictionary of Old Testament Theology and Exegesis, Volume 4,* (Grand Rapids, MI: Zondervan Publishing House, 1997), 896.

7. This reality reminds one of the famous maxims of the early Church theologian Augustine: "The New is in the Old concealed, the Old is in the New revealed." Others have said it this way: "The New is in the Old contained, the Old is by the New explained." For our purposes we might say: "What is latent in the Old becomes patent in the New." Or "Subsequent revelation often makes explicit what was implicit in antecedent revelation."

8. It will be shown below that the Old Covenant includes the whole of Mosaic legislation, not merely the Decalogue.

New Covenant include the writing of the Decalogue on the hearts of God's people.[9] "The [torah] is . . . the Decalogue. . . ."[10]

We are now prepared to note that the change is not from one law to another law, but from stone to hearts. The text of Jeremiah clearly teaches that the basic, fundamental law of God under the New Covenant is the Decalogue.[11] What God does is write it on the hearts of all covenant citizens. It is not the Ten Commandments as Old Covenant law that is being referred to, but as New Covenant law. There is *discontinuity* and *continuity*. There is *continuity* of law—the Ten Commandments,[12] and *discontinuity* of place—stone to hearts.

Just as it is important to notice what the text does say, it is equally important to observe what the text does not say. The text does not say that the law of God under the New Covenant consists of a disposition to obey. This is something true of saved Old Covenant saints and would not be anything new. A disposition to obey is *one* of the promised blessings of the New Covenant, according to Ezekiel 11:19, which says, "Then I will give them one heart, and I will put a new spirit within them, and take the stony heart out of their flesh, and give them a heart of flesh. . . ." What will be the disposition of this new heart? Ezekiel 11:20 tells us: "that they may walk in My statutes and keep My judgments and do them . . ."[13]. Ezekiel 36:26–27 promise the same thing

---

9. This understanding of Jeremiah 31:33 was held by Thomas Boston in the eighteenth century. See Edward Fisher, *The Marrow of Modern Divinity*, (Edmonton, AB Canada: Still Waters Revival Books, re. 1991), 177.

10. William McKane, *A Critical and Exegetical Commentary on Jeremiah, Volume II*, (Edinburgh, Scotland: T&T Clark, 1996), 820.

11. This in no way infers that the Decalogue has the corner on law under the New Covenant. See the comments on Hebrews 8:10 above. The Decalogue summarily contains the Moral Law, not exhausts it.

12. Some might want to challenge the approach here, which reduces torah to the Decalogue. However, not reducing torah to the Decalogue produces the difficulty of answering the question why God would write temporary, ceremonial laws that point to Christ on the hearts of New Covenant people *after* Christ's work on the cross abrogated those very laws.

13. Common synonyms for the Hebrew word *law* (*torah*) in the Old Testament include: statutes, ordinances, precepts, judgments, My (God's) voice, and My (God's) word.

in slightly different language. The promise of the New Covenant includes both a *law* to follow and a *disposition* of heart to obey. The phrase "My law" in Jeremiah *never* refers to a disposition in men but always and clearly to something revealed by God to Israel as His Old Covenant nation. In fact, the Hebrew word for law, *torah*, used by Jeremiah, is mentioned 305 other times in the Hebrew Old Testament and never refers to a human disposition.[14]

And, as we have seen, the text also does not say that the law of God under the New Covenant consists of a new law. The *Word Biblical Commentary* says, "There is no indication . . . that the content of the law, God's will revealed in commandment, statute, and ordinance, will be altered in the new covenant."[15] Kaiser agrees, when he says, "When the items of continuity in the New covenant are tabulated in this passage, they are: (1) the same covenant-making God, 'My covenant'; (2) the same law, 'My torah' (note, not a different one than Sinai). . . ."[16] A new law is not being referred to, but a new covenant, *the* New Covenant, and even a new place for the law of God to be written— the hearts of *all* covenant citizens, instead of on stone tablets.

This brings up a question worth pursuing before going on. What exactly is new about the New Covenant?[17] Pieter A. Verhoef comments.

> The basic issue is whether the "new covenant" must be conceived of as radically new, as totally different from the old,

---

14. The word *law* (*torah*) is used 306 times in the Hebrew text in 214 verses. It normally refers to the law revealed by God through Moses to Israel. It does have other uses, but never referring to a disposition of the heart. Its uses include: the law of the Old Covenant as a whole, the book of the covenant, the Decalogue, the words of a prophet, the providence of God, and the instruction of parents.

15. Gerald L. Keown, Pamela J. Scalise, and Thomas G. Smothers, *Word Biblical Commentary, Volume 27, Jeremiah 26–52*, (Dallas, TX: Word Books, Publisher, 1995), 134. It should be noted that the authors define *law* (*torah*) in Jeremiah 31:33 more generically than I do.

16. Kaiser, *Toward an Old Testament Theology*, 233.

17. The Hebrew word for *new* (*hadash*) can refer to the concept of renewing, repairing, or making something fresh. See R. Laird Harris, Gleason

Sinaitic covenant. It is obvious that there are a number of similarities that suggest an element of continuity: both are being concluded by God, both are made with Israel, both concern the compliance with the torah, and both have the same purpose; to enhance the covenant relationship between God and his people. . . . [18]

The newness of the New Covenant can be seen in at least four ways from Jeremiah's prophecy. First, unlike the Old Covenant, the New Covenant cannot be broken. This is what Jeremiah means in verse 32, when he says, "not according to the covenant that I made with their fathers in the day that I took them by the hand to lead them out of the land of Egypt, My covenant which they broke, though I was a husband to them, says the Lord." There is obvious antithesis, or discontinuity, here between the violability of the Old Covenant and the inviolability of the New Covenant.[19]

Second, unlike the Old Covenant, the law of God will be put in the minds and written on the hearts of all covenant citizens (verse 33).[20] Under the Old Covenant, the basic, fundamental law of the covenant, the Ten Commandments, was written on

---

L. Archer, Bruce K. Waltke, *Theological Wordbook of the Old Testament, Volume I*, (Chicago, IL: Moody Press, 1980), 265–266. Some Old Testament scholars argue that the word *new* means renewed in the context of Jeremiah 31:31–34. They argue from this meaning of the word for both *continuity* and *discontinuity* between the Old and New Covenants. For instance, Kaiser says, "Thus the word 'new' in this context would mean the 'renewed' or 'restored' covenant." Kaiser, *Toward an Old Testament Theology*, 234. Kaiser and others view the New Covenant as administrating the Old Testament covenant promises in a new way. See also O. Palmer Robertson, *The Christ of the Covenants*, (Phillipsburg, NJ: Presbyterian and Reformed Publishing Company, 1980, re. 1985), 280–286.

18. Willem A. Van Gemeren, General Editor, *New International Dictionary of Old Testament Theology and Exegesis, Volume 2*, (Grand Rapids, MI: Zondervan Publishing House, 1997), 35.

19. See Deuteronomy 29:25–28; Jeremiah 11:9–10, 22:6–9, 34:13–14; Ezekiel 44:6–8; and Psalm 78:10–11 for texts which teach that the Old Covenant was breakable and broken.

20. See Psalm 37:31 and Isaiah 51:7 for evidence that the law was on the heart of at least some Old Covenant citizens.

tablets of stone. Under the New Covenant, the basic, fundamental law of the covenant will be written on tablets of flesh, of the heart.

Third, unlike the Old Covenant, everyone in the New Covenant will know the Lord (verse 34a). This was not so under the Old Covenant. One could be in the Old Covenant and not know the Lord savingly.[21]

Fourth, unlike the Old Covenant, everyone in the New Covenant will have their sins forgiven (verse 34b).

With these features of the newness of the New Covenant understood, it becomes quite clear that any form of neonomianism[22] cannot be read *out of* the text of Jeremiah. All forms of neonomianism are read *into* the text, but neocovenantalism is read *out of* the text.[23] In other words, there is an explicit continuity of basic, fundamental law being referred to by Jeremiah. Based on the words of Jeremiah, we are to expect at least a degree of ethical continuity between the Old and New Covenants.

And finally, the text does not say that the law of God under the New Covenant consists of a heretofore unrevealed, transcendent law. This is completely foreign to the text and the rest of the book of Jeremiah. The simple reading of the text argues for another understanding than the ones just mentioned.

---

21. See 2 Samuel 2:12 where Eli's sons are said to "not know the LORD." Surely they knew *about* the Lord. What they did not have was the *saving* knowledge of God, though they were citizens of the Old Covenant.

22. Newlawism.

23. Those who reduce the newness of the New Covenant to a new law cannot adequately deal with the newness stipulated here by Jeremiah. As well, those who reduce the phrase Old Covenant to equal the Decalogue are forced to conclude that the phrase New Covenant means a New Decalogue. The Old Covenant is simply called "the covenant" in the Old Testament. If "the covenant" equals the Decalogue, then Jeremiah would be promising a new Decalogue. This reminds one of Martin Luther's statements that Christ and His apostles established "new decalogues." He goes on to say that "these decalogues are clearer than the decalogue of Moses, just as the countenance of Christ is brighter than the countenance of Moses (2 Corinthians 3:7–11)." Cited in Paul Althaus, *The Ethics of Martin Luther*, (Philadelphia, PA: Fortress Press, 1972), 30–31.

Challenge to New Covenant Theology

The standard New Covenant Theology interpretation of Jeremiah 31:33 puts an unnecessary wedge between the Ten Commandments as a unit and New Covenant ethics. This forces New Covenant Theology to impose something on the New Testament from the Old Testament that is simply not there. Jeremiah is not teaching us that the New Covenant will be the death knell of the Decalogue as a unit.[24] To the contrary, he is teaching us that the New Covenant is the death knell of the Old Covenant. The basic, fundamental law of the Old Covenant is assumed into the New Covenant, not replaced by it, according to Jeremiah.

---

24. Not identifying the law written on the heart as the Decalogue is one way New Covenant theologians avoid the abiding validity of the Sabbath, the fourth commandment, under the New Covenant.

2

New Covenant Theology and the Identity of the Old Covenant

The Issue at Stake

A second area of challenge for New Covenant Theology concerns the identity of the Old Covenant. According to New Covenant Theology, the Old Covenant is identified as the Ten Commandments, the Decalogue. New Covenant theologian Fred Zaspel says, "The Decalogue *is* the statement of the [old] covenant."[1] He then adds, "Indeed, God Himself says so."[2] After quoting Exodus 34:27–28, he says:

> Much hermeneutical and theological confusion has resulted from a failure to appreciate this identification. The ten words to Israel *are* the covenant; apart from this foundational summary statement (the Decalogue), there is no covenant at all.[3]

Likewise, John Reisinger identifies the Old Covenant as the Ten Commandments. In *Christ, Lord and Lawgiver Over the Church*, he says, "Under the old covenant (Tablets of Stone), polygamy was not a sin."[4] In *But I Say Unto You*, he says, "[The]

---

1. Zaspel, "Divine Law," 149.
2. *Ibid.*
3. *Ibid.*
4. John G. Reisinger, *Christ, Lord and Lawgiver Over the Church*, (Frederick, MD: New Covenant Media, 1998), 18.

New Covenant replaced the Old Covenant (Tablets of Stone) given at Sinai. . . ."[5]

Reisinger's book, *Tablets of Stone*, attempts to "study the place and function of the Ten Commandments in redemptive history as this plan unfolds in the OT Scriptures, moves into the NT Scriptures, and finally reaches into the life of the Church today."[6] In this important work, Reisinger argues extensively that the Ten Commandments equal the Old Covenant. He states that, when we think of the Ten Commandments, "[w]e are *always* [emphasis added] to think 'Old Covenant.'"[7] His chapter titles bear this out clearly. Chapters three through five and eight are entitled as follows: "The Ten Commandments Are A 'Covenant'"; "The Ten Commandments Are A 'Legal' Covenant"; "The Ten Commandments Were Given to the Nation of Israel"; and "The Tablets of Stone, or Ten Commandments, As a Covenant Document, Had a Historical Beginning and a Historical End." In Reisinger's summary of the final chapter of the book, he says, "The Bible always considers the Tablets of Stone (Ten Commandments) as the specific covenant document that established the nation of Israel as a body politic at Mt. Sinai."[8] "The Scripture nowhere states or infers that we are to think of the Tablets of Stone as 'God's eternal unchanging moral law.' We are always to think 'Old Covenant.'"[9]

To be sure, Reisinger himself contradicts this statement, when he says, "The Ten Commandments, *as interpreted and applied by Christ,* are a very important part of the Christian's rule of life."[10] How can we think of the Ten Commandments as exclusively Old Covenant and *as a very important part of the Christian's rule of life* at the same time? This appears to be a case where even New Covenant Theology concedes that the Ten Commandments, at least in some sense, transcend the Old

---

5. Reisinger, *But I Say Unto You*, 27.
6. Reisinger, *Tablets of Stone*, Author's Preface, no pagination.
7. *Ibid*, 99.
8. *Ibid*.
9. *Ibid*.
10. *Ibid*, 99–100. Unless noted, all emphases in John Reisinger quotes are his.

Covenant.[11] Reisinger's last assertion is in complete agreement with the historic Reformed position, though he obviously does not mean what Reformed theology means by it. Back to our question. Is the New Covenant Theology position correct? Does the Bible identify the Old Covenant as consisting only of the Ten Commandments? Did the Ten Commandments have a historical beginning (at Sinai) and a historical end (at the cross)? Is it true that Scripture nowhere states or infers that the Ten Commandments function any other way than as God's covenant with Israel, the Old Covenant? Is it true that when the Bible speaks of the Decalogue, it always refers to it as the Old Covenant in its entirety? In analyzing this aspect of New Covenant Theology, let's take these claims to the bar of Scripture and see if these things are so.

It must be admitted that, at first blush, New Covenant Theology appears to have a strong case for identifying the Old Covenant as the Ten Commandments. Exodus 34:27–28 says, "Then the LORD said to Moses, 'Write these words, for according to the tenor of these words I have made a covenant with you and with Israel.' So he was there with the LORD forty days and forty nights; he neither ate bread nor drank water. And He wrote on the tablets the words of the covenant, the Ten Commandments." Commenting on this text, John Reisinger asserts, "Exodus 34:27–28 gives us the key to the nature and function of their [the Ten Commandments] use in the history of redemption."[12] Obviously, he must take this view since defining the Old Covenant as the Ten Commandments is fundamental to New Covenant Theology's understanding of the relationship between the Covenants and the place of the Ten Commandments in the history of redemption and Christian ethics.

---

11. I believe New Covenant theologians would seek to avoid this dilemma by claiming that some of the individual commands in the Ten Commandments do transcend the Old Covenant, but the Ten Commandments as a unit do not. This will be discussed below.

12. Reisinger, *Tablets of Stone*, 99.

How the Bible Identifies the Old Covenant

There are at least two Old Testament texts, Jeremiah 34:13–14 and Ezekiel 44:6–8, and two New Testament texts, Hebrews 9:1 and 9:18, which clearly refute the New Covenant Theology equation that the Ten Commandments equal the Old Covenant.

JEREMIAH 34:13–14[13]

Consider Jeremiah 34:13–14, which reads:

> Thus says the LORD, the God of Israel: "I made a covenant with your fathers in the day that I brought them out of the land of Egypt, out of the house of bondage, saying, 'At the end of seven years let every man set free his Hebrew brother, who has been sold to him; and when he has served you six years, you shall let him go free from you.' But your fathers did not obey Me nor incline their ear."

In the book of Jeremiah, the covenant God made with the fathers in the day He brought them out of the land of Egypt is the Old Covenant (see Jer. 31:32). According to this text, the Old Covenant was violated when they transgressed the *civil laws* concerning Hebrew slavery. Since those laws are not found in the Ten Commandments, then the phrase "Old Covenant" is not interchangeable with the phrase "Ten Commandments." It is clear that this text views the covenant God made with Israel, the Old Covenant, as *not* strictly identifiable with the Ten Commandments.

EZEKIEL 44:6–8

Consider next Ezekiel 44:6–8, which reads:

> Now say to the rebellious, to the house of Israel, "Thus says the LORD God: 'O house of Israel, let Us have no more of your

---

13. The following comments on Jeremiah and Ezekiel are a paraphrase of thoughts relayed to me by a friend of mine, Greg Welty. They were extracted by permission from an email discussion he had with a New Covenant theologian.

abominations. When you brought in foreigners, uncircumcised in heart and uncircumcised in flesh, to be in My sanctuary to defile it—My house—and when you offered My food, the fat and the blood, then they broke My covenant because of all your abominations. And you have not kept charge of My holy things, but you have set *others* to keep charge of My sanctuary for you.'"

According to this text, the Israelites were the cause of God's covenant being broken by transgressing the *ceremonial laws* concerning bringing uncircumcised foreigners into the sanctuary. Since those laws are not found in the Ten Commandments, then the phrase "Old Covenant" is not interchangeable with the phrase "Ten Commandments." Accordingly, this text also refutes the notion that the Old Covenant is to be equated with the Ten Commandments.

HEBREWS **9:1**

Both New Testament texts that refute New Covenant Theology's contention that the Old Covenant *is* the Ten Commandments are in Hebrews. In Hebrews 9:1, we read, "Then indeed, even the first covenant had ordinances of divine service and the earthly sanctuary." In the context of the book of Hebrews, the first Covenant always refers to the covenant God made with Israel, the Old Covenant, which has been replaced by the New Covenant (see Heb. 8:7, 13, and 9:1). According to New Covenant Theology, this verse would read, "Then indeed, even the Ten Commandments had ordinances of divine service and the earthly sanctuary." But, did the Decalogue of itself have "ordinances of divine service and the earthly sanctuary"? No, it did not. The "ordinances of divine service and the earthly sanctuary" are not included in the Decalogue at all.

The point should be clear that the author of Hebrews does not understand the first Covenant as referring exclusively to the Ten Commandments, but to the whole of the Mosaic legislation. The Old Covenant *includes* the Ten Commandments, but is *not exhausted* by them. John Reisinger uses this text to try to prove that the Decalogue, the first Covenant, according to New

Covenant Theology, is separate from the ordinances of divine service and the earthly sanctuary. Watch what he does while quoting this text. *"Now the* **first covenant** *had regulations for worship (Don't confuse the actual covenant, the Ten Commandments, with all the "regulations"). . . ."*[14] But it has already been shown that two of God's prophets do the very thing Reisinger wants us not to do. Both Jeremiah and Ezekiel saw the Old Covenant as inclusive of ceremonial and civil laws. Reisinger's understanding of Hebrews 9:1, therefore, is stained with a presupposition that cannot be established, and which, in fact, is clearly refuted by the Bible's own understanding of what constitutes the Old Covenant.

HEBREWS **9:18**
In Hebrew 9:18, we read, "Therefore not even the first covenant was dedicated without blood." In other words, the first Covenant, the Old Covenant, is viewed as being dedicated or inaugurated by the shedding of blood. According to *The New Linguistic and Exegetical Key to the Greek New Testament,* the word translated *dedicated* in the NKJV means ". . . to renew, to dedicate. The idea of the word is to introduce something new, to initiate, w[ith] the concepts of inauguration and dedication closely related. . . ."[15] The point is that Hebrews 9:18 sees the inauguration of the first Covenant, the Old Covenant, transpiring in Exodus 24, where offerings were made, not Exodus 20, where the Ten Commandments were given. The revelation of the Decalogue does not constitute the totality of the Old Covenant. The Decalogue, the Book of the Covenant, and the blood of the Covenant all go together (see Exod. 24:1–8). Therefore, the Old Covenant must include more than the Decalogue and was not wholly inaugurated at Sinai at the giving of the Ten Commandments.

---

14. Reisinger, *Tablets of Stone,* 71.
15. Cleon L. Rogers, Jr. & Cleon L. Rogers, III, *The New Linguistic and Exegetical Key to the Greek New Testament,* (Grand Rapids, MI: Zondervan Publishing House, 1998), 536.

EXPOSITION OF EXODUS 34:27–28[16]

It should be obvious by now that Jeremiah 34:13–14, Ezekiel 44:6–8, and Hebrews 9:1 and 18 are biblical commentaries upon the Old Covenant, which clearly identify that Covenant with things *outside* of the Decalogue. The conclusion we draw from these verses is that the New Covenant Theology equation over-simplifies the issue. One text, Exodus 34:27–28, is taken to be *the key* to the nature and function of the Ten Commandments throughout Scripture. However, Scripture itself does not warrant such an equation.

Indeed, Exodus 34:27–28 itself appears to argue against such an equation. These verses come in the context of God renewing the covenant with Israel. Israel had broken the covenant by committing idolatry with the golden calf in Exodus 32. In Exodus 34:1, God says to Moses, "Cut two tablets of stone like the first *ones*, and I will write on *these* tablets the words that were on the first tablets which you broke." Moses obeyed the Lord, as Exodus 34:4 says, "So he cut two tablets of stone like the first *ones*. Then Moses rose early in the morning and went up Mount Sinai, as the LORD had commanded him; and he took in his hand the two tablets of stone." In verses 5 through 7, the Lord proclaims His name to Moses. In verses 8 and 9, Moses responds in humble adoration and prayer for pardon for Israel. In verses 10 through 26, the terms of the renewed covenant are given. In Exodus 34:10, the Lord says, "Behold, I make a covenant." Commenting on this statement, George Bush says, "Indeed upon an attentive view of the whole context we can scarcely consider it as any thing short of an actual and formal renewal of the covenant which the people had broken. . . ."[17] The covenant was already inaugurated with blood in Exodus 24. Therefore, here in Exodus 34, the same covenant is renewed, though without the shedding of

16. I owe the following observation to a friend of mine, Tim Etherington. He made this point while discussing Exodus 34:27–28 with a New Covenant theologian.
17. George Bush, *Commentary on Exodus*, (Grand Rapids, MI: Kregel Publications, re. 1993), 547.

blood. Exodus 34:27 contains God's concluding words to Moses while on Sinai. God says, "Write *these words* [emphasis added], for according to the tenor of these words I have made a covenant with you and with Israel."

What does the noun phrase, "these words," refer to? It refers to the words contained in verses 10 through 26. Listen to Bush again.

> What then were the words which Moses wrote? Certainly that summary of judicial and ceremonial precepts comprised in the verses immediately preceding from v. 11th to v. 26th, which were an appendage to the moral law, and which formed, in all their details, the conditions of the national covenant on the part of the nation.[18]

What Moses wrote was verses 10 through 26. What God wrote was the second edition of the Decalogue on the second set of stone tablets (see Deut. 10:1–5). Exodus 34:28 contains Moses' concluding words to us concerning what happened while on Sinai. He says, "So he [Moses] was there with the LORD forty days and forty nights; he neither ate bread nor drank water. And He [the LORD] wrote on the tablets the words of the covenant, the Ten Commandments." While Moses was on Sinai, God wrote the Ten Commandments on the stone tablets. Either while on Sinai or some time afterward, Moses wrote the contents of Exodus 34:10–26, which became a part of the covenant with Israel. Exodus 34:27–28, New Covenant Theology's key text, thus negates New Covenant Theology's identification of the Old Covenant as the Ten Commandments.

Challenge to New Covenant Theology

The lesson to learn from all this is that defining terms by the questionable understanding of one text or one word often spells trouble. For instance, using New Covenant Theology's method of defining the Old Covenant, it would be true that the phrase "New Covenant" is exhausted by "I will put My law in their

---

18. Bush, *Exodus*, 552.

minds, and write it on their hearts; and I will be their God, and they shall be My people" or other biblical synonyms of Jeremiah 31:33. Jeremiah does start out verse 33 by saying, "But this *is* the covenant. . . ." Supposing this be the case, how would we explain Luke 22:20 and 1 Corinthians 11:25, which both say, ". . . this cup *is* the new covenant"? Which is the New Covenant? The law written on the heart or the cup? New Covenant Theology makes the word *is* mean *equals* (Old Covenant=Ten Commandments), with no room for future elaboration. If this were so, the New Covenant could not equal both the law written on the heart and the cup. Yet both are true.

How can this be? The answer lies in allowing the copula, the verb *to be*, to take on its specific nuance according to use in context. For instance, "This is My body . . ." means "this *represents* My body." The bread is a visible representation of another reality. By forcing the word *is* to mean *equals*, New Covenant Theology ends up avoiding the rest of the Bible's comments on the identity of the Old Covenant and function of the Ten Commandments in subsequent redemptive history. This is not an adequate hermeneutic.

The Function of the Ten Commandments Outside the Old Covenant

This brings us to a most important question: Does the Bible view the Ten Commandments *as a unit,* functioning any other way than as Old Covenant law? New Covenant Theology affirms that the Ten Commandments never function outside the Old Covenant as a unit. It claims that "The Bible always relates the Ten Commandments to Israel at Mt. Sinai."[19] John Reisinger is careful to say, "We are only insisting that when the Ten Commandments are considered *as a single unit* [emphasis added], as the 'Tablets of Stone,' they are always viewed as a '*covenant.*'"[20] This qualification allows New Covenant theologians to acknowledge that the Tablets of Stone contain much moral law. Zaspel

---

19. Reisinger, *Tablets of Stone,* 16.
20. *Ibid,* 88.

says, "Idolatry, murder, theft, adultery, etc., did not first become
wrong when Israel was at Sinai. The great bulk of the Decalogue, then, is clearly but a formal codification of the law of
God that was (and is) in man's heart naturally."[21] Reisinger even
goes so far as to say, "The Ten Commandments contain much
unchanging moral law that is just as binding on us today as it
was on an Israelite."[22] However, due to New Covenant Theology's
pre-commitment to the equation that the Old Covenant equals
the Ten Commandments, under that view, the Ten Commandments, *as a unit*, can no longer function as covenant law for
God's New Covenant people.

Several biblical passages are to the contrary. We have already
seen that Jeremiah 31:33 refers to the Ten Commandments functioning as a unit under the New Covenant. Three New Testament texts, 2 Corinthians 3:3, Ephesians 6:2–3, and 1 Timothy
1:8–11 also demonstrate that the Ten Commandments do indeed function outside of the Old Covenant and as a unit.[23]

EXPOSITION OF 2 CORINTHIANS 3:3

Second Corinthians 3:3 reads: "clearly you are an epistle of
Christ, ministered by us, written not with ink but by the Spirit
of the living God, not on tablets of stone but on tablets of flesh,
that is, of the heart." The section begins in 2:17 as an extended
argument for the validity of Paul's ministry. In 3:1 Paul offers a
regulating question, "do we need, as some others, epistles of
commendation to you or letters of commendation from you?"
In 3:2 Paul uses a metaphor depicting the Corinthians themselves as a letter written on his heart. In 3:3 he uses a similar
metaphor for a different purpose, stating that the Corinthian
believers "are an epistle of Christ, ministered by us, written not
with ink but by the Spirit of the living God, not on tablets of
stone but on tablets of flesh, that is, of the heart."

Consider the following observations about verse 3.

---

21. Zaspel, "Divine Law," 148.
22. Reisinger, *Tablets of Stone*, 89.
23. Matthew 5:17–20; Romans 2:14–15, 3:19–20; and Second Timothy
3:16–17 establish this as well.

First, in the context, Paul is obviously talking about the New Covenant as prophesied by Jeremiah.[24] This assertion is proved by the language used by Paul in verse 6, "new covenant", and in verse 3 where the parallels with Jeremiah 31:33 are striking. John Calvin says, "He alludes to the promise that is recorded in Jer. xxxi. 31, and Ezek. xxxvii. [sic] 26, concerning the grace of the New Testament. . . . Paul says, that this blessing was accomplished through means of his preaching."[25]

Second, Christ is the author of this epistle written on the heart. The phrase "of Christ" is best understood as a subjective genitive, which makes Christ the author of the epistle written on the heart. This adds weight to Paul's argument in context. He is combating false teachers and seeking to defend his ministry. Christ authenticates Paul's ministry by doing the work only God can do in writing upon the souls of men. There is in this text a witness to the doctrine of the deity of Christ, when understood as referring to Jeremiah 31:33.

Third, Christ, the Divine author uses not ink, but the Holy Spirit to write on the hearts of men.

Fourth, the tablets of stone refers to the Ten Commandments as originally written by God (see 2 Cor. 3:7 and Exod. 31:18).

Fifth, the tablets of flesh (the heart) refers to the Corinthians.

Sixth, unlike the writing on tablets of stone under the Old Covenant, which was a ministry of death, the writing on the tablets of hearts under the New Covenant is a ministry of the Spirit, which gives life (see verses 6–7).

Seventh, assuming Paul has Jeremiah's prophecy in mind, what Christ writes on the heart is the law of God as promised in Jeremiah 31:33. Colin Kruse comments:

At the end of the verse [verse 3], while furthering his argument, Paul varies the metaphor by saying this letter writing was carried out not *on tablets of stone but on tablets of human*

---

24. Paul could as well have thoughts of Ezekiel 11 and 36 in his mind. However, since he uses the phrase "new covenant" in 3:6, it seems that he has at least Jeremiah 31 in mind.

25. John Calvin, *Calvin's Commentaries, Volume XX*, (Grand Rapids, MI: Baker Book House, re. 1984), 168.

hearts. Here Paul leaves behind the contrast between the work of a scribe using pen and ink and the work of an apostle ministering in the power of the Spirit, and introduces another contrast, that between writing on tablets of stone and on human hearts. This latter contrast is clearly an illusion to the prophetic description of the new covenant (*cf.* Jer. 31:31–34; Ezk. 36:24–32) under which God would write his law on human hearts.[26]

It is important to see that Paul shifts the metaphor at the end of verse 3. He goes from what the Corinthians are to him in verse 2, "our epistle written on our hearts," to what Christ did in the Corinthians to make them Paul's epistle. *The Cambridge Testament for Schools and Colleges* says:

> [T]he proverbial opposition between "hearts of flesh" and "hearts of stone" (Ezek. xi. 19, xxxvi. 26; Jer. xxxi. 33) comes into his mind, together with the thought of God's writing His law formerly on tables of stone, now on tables which are hearts of flesh.[27]

Paul's ministry is in fulfillment of Old Testament prophecy. The movement in Paul's thought is not from one law to no law or to a totally new law, but the same law from *stone* to *heart.* Philip Hughes gives these helpful comments in his commentary on 2 Corinthians.

> It is evident that Paul has in mind the contrast between the giving of the law to Moses on Mount Sinai and the establishment of the new covenant prophesied by Jeremiah. At Sinai the law had been written by the finger of God on tablets of stone (Ex. 31:18); but this was an external law-giving, whereby sinful man was confronted with his awful inability to fulfill the just requirements of his holy Creator. Jer. 31:33, however, promises a law-giving that is internal,

---

26. Colin Kruse, *The Second epistle of Paul to the Corinthians,* (Grand Rapids, MI: Wm. B. Eerdmans Company, 1987, re. 1997), 91.

27. Alfred Plummer, editor, *Cambridge Greek Testament for Schools and Colleges: The Second Epistle of Paul the Apostle to the Corinthians,* (London, England: Cambridge University Press, 1912), 57.

namely, the writing by God of His law in the very heart itself. It is most important to realize that it is the selfsame law which was graven on tables of stone at Sinai that in this age of the new covenant is graven on the tables of the human heart by the Holy Spirit. The gospel does not abrogate the law, but fulfills it. There is no question, as Augustine points out, of Paul finding fault with the dispensation of the Old Testament. The Christian is still under solemn obligation to keep the law of God, but with this vital difference, that he now has the power, the power of Christ by the Holy Spirit within himself, to keep it. The law, therefore, is neither evil nor obsolete, but, as Paul says elsewhere, "the law is holy, and the commandment holy, and righteous, and good" (Rom. 7:12). Nor is the law opposed to love; on the contrary, love of God and love of one's neighbor are the sum of the law, as our Lord Himself taught (Mk. 12:28–31): love, the Apostle affirms, is precisely "the fulfillment of the law" (Rom. 13:8–10).[28]

Elsewhere, Hughes adds, "The establishment of the new covenant, however, implies neither the abrogation nor the deprecation of the Mosaic Law. . . . There is no question of a *new law* or of *no law*. Neither God changes nor His law."[29] It could be added that there is no question of the law changing from an objective, definable ethical code to a subjective, undefinable disposition of the heart or to a totally unrevealed, transcendent law. Paul and Jeremiah agree. Geoffrey Wilson says:

> The superiority of the new covenant over the old dispensation is not that it sets aside the decalogue (the moral law), but that it transfers that law from tablets of stone to "tables that are hearts of flesh" [cf. Ezek. 11.19; 36.26]. This is the fulfillment of Jeremiah's prophecy, "I will put *my law* in their inward parts, and in their heart will I write it" [Jer 31.33].[30]

Paul's understanding of the law of God written on the heart under the New Covenant from 2 Corinthians 3:3 now becomes

28. Philip Edgcumbe Hughes, *Paul's Second Epistle to the Corinthians*, (Grand Rapids, MI: Wm. B. Eerdmans Publishing Co., 1962, re. 1986), 89–90.

29. *Ibid*, 94.

30. Geoffrey B. Wilson, *2 Corinthians, A Digest of Reformed Comment*, (Carlisle, PA: The Banner of Truth Trust, 1979), 41.

clear. That law is the Ten Commandments, the fundamental, basic law of the Old Covenant. The function of the Ten Commandments under the New Covenant is similar to their function under the Old in some senses, albeit dissimilar in others. There is *continuity* and *discontinuity*. The Ten Commandments were and are educational in terms of showing the righteousness of God, man's duty, and, due to the presence of sin in man, his inability to keep them. However, for the Christian, the citizen of the New Covenant, the condemnatory function of the Ten Commandments no longer applies. Christ was condemned for his sins once for all at Calvary. Praise the Lord! However, they still function as the fundamental pattern for righteous living.

Granted, the application of the Ten Commandments under the New Covenant differs from their application under the Old. However, a shift in application does not mean a shift in fundamental, basic, Moral Law. Second Corinthians 3:3 is one New Testament text that assumes the abiding validity of the Decalogue outside of the Old Covenant as a unit.

EXPOSITION OF EPHESIANS 6:2–3

Ephesians 6:2–3 is another text which assumes that the Ten Commandments function outside of the Old Covenant as a unit. In Ephesians 6:2–3 we read, "'Honor your father and mother,' which is the first commandment with promise: 'that it may be well with you and you may live long on the earth.'" Several observations will help us in order to understand how this passage assumes that the Ten Commandments function outside of the Old Covenant as a unit.

First, the fifth commandment of the Decalogue is introduced as support that obedience to parents is right. Benjamin B. Warfield notes, "The acknowledged authority of the fifth commandment as such in the Christian Church is simply taken for granted."[31] Paul does not qualify his use of this Old Testament text or explain the basis for using it; he simply assumes its authoritative relevance.

31. Benjamin B. Warfield, *Selected Shorter Writings of Benjamin B. Warfield, I,* (Phillipsburg, NJ: Presbyterian and Reformed Publishing Company, 1970), 322.

Second, the fifth commandment is introduced as the first commandment with promise. He did not say "the first that is morally binding," "the first in the Bible," "the first in the New Testament," or "the first in this epistle." It is clear that he is referring to the fifth commandment as it appears elsewhere in a series of commands in which it is *the first in that series* with a promise. The only place this occurs in the entire Bible is in the Decalogue, the Ten Commandments.[32]

Third, Paul views the Decalogue as a whole unit and in a positive light. If the fifth commandment is applicable in a positive way, and if Paul is assuming it as it occurred in a series of commandments in which it was the first with a promise, then the commands which precede and follow it still function as commands in a series.

Fourth, the promise stated is applied to children in Asia Minor in the first century. If the command applies, then certainly its promise does as well. This shows us that there may be elements within the Decalogue, as originally given, that applied specifically to Israel as God's Old Covenant nation and that now

---

32. Many commentators acknowledge the fact that Paul is referring to the fifth commandment as it appears in the Decalogue. See for example John Eadie, *Commentary on the Epistle to the Ephesians*, (Minneapolis, MN: James and Klock Christian Publishing Co., re. 1977), 438–443; and Andrew T. Lincoln, *Word Biblical Commentary: Ephesians*, (Dallas, TX: Word Books, Publisher, 1990), 404–406. Some deny that Paul is referring to the fifth commandment as it is found in the Decalogue because the second commandment seems to have a promise attached to it that would obviously mean Paul could not have been referring to the Decalogue. Andrew Lincoln clears up this apparent difficulty in the following words: "How can the fifth commandment be said to be the first commandment with a promise, when the second commandment in Exod. 20:4–6 also appears to include a promise about God showing steadfast love to those who love him and keep his commandments? . . . Strictly speaking, the words 'but showing steadfast love to thousands of those who love me and keep my commandments' in Exod. 20:6 are not a promise connected with 'you shall not make for yourself a graven image' in Exod 20:4, but are the positive side of the description of Yahweh as a jealous God which follows in Exod 20:5. It is not surprising, therefore, for Exod 20:12 to be thought of as the first commandment with a promise." Lincoln, *Ephesians*, 404. See also the section in Eadie as noted above, especially where Eadie deals with the issue of the fifth commandment being the *first* with a promise, which seems to imply more after it with promises.

apply to the Church under the New Covenant. This promise originally referred to the Promised Land of the Abrahamic Covenant. In one sense, it was originally restricted to that same Promised Land. However, the utility of the Decalogue transcends the Promised Land under the New Covenant. This shows us that the Decalogue is still binding as a unit under the New Covenant, though not in the same manner in which it was under the Old. The law is the same; its application is modified to fit the conditions brought in by the death of Christ and the inauguration of the New Covenant.

By the way, there is nothing in Paul's language which suggests that the fifth commandment is binding, simply because it is repeated. This is often a hermeneutical presupposition used by those who deny the utility of the Decalogue as such under the New Covenant. It cannot be borne out by exegesis.

Let us now tie in how this text indicates that the Ten Commandments function outside the Old Covenant as a unit. The Decalogue was given as and is always assumed to be "an inseparable unit"[33] in the Old Testament under the Old Covenant. Jeremiah assumes this in Jeremiah 31:33. Paul assumes the same thing in both 2 Corinthians 3 and here in Ephesians 6. However, he assumes this *after* the Old Covenant had been replaced by the New Covenant. So even after the New Covenant replaces the Old Covenant, the Ten Commandments are viewed as a unit outside of the Old Covenant and in a prescriptively positive context. What we have then is the fruit of Jeremiah's prophecy of not only the writing of the law of God on the heart (2 Cor. 3:3), but the application of the fifth commandment in such a way that assumes the relevance of the whole Decalogue in a positive light with a modified application (Eph. 6:2–3). This is exactly what is expected from the Old Testament. This not only supports the unity of the Bible, but the basic unity of ethics, Old or New Covenant. The Ten Commandments are, therefore, transcovenantal. Ephesians 6:2–3 is another New Testament text which assumes the

---

33. Zaspel, "Divine Law", 155. I agree with New Covenant Theology on this point.

abiding validity of the Decalogue outside of the Old Covenant as a unit.

EXPOSITION OF 1 TIMOTHY 1:8–11

A final New Testament text that assumes that the Ten Commandments function outside the Old Covenant as a unit is 1 Timothy 1:8–11. There, we read:

> But we know that the law is good if one uses it lawfully, knowing this: that the law is not made for a righteous person, but for *the* lawless and insubordinate, for *the* ungodly and for sinners, for *the* unholy and profane, for murderers of fathers and murderers of mothers, for manslayers, for fornicators, for sodomites, for kidnappers, for liars, for perjurers, and if there is any other thing that is contrary to sound doctrine, according to the glorious gospel of the blessed God which was committed to my trust.

In considering this passage, four questions will be asked to frame the outline for its exposition. 1) Why does Paul bring up the issue of the law? 2) What is said about the law? 3) To whom is Paul referring when he says, "the law is not made for a righteous person"? 4) What law is Paul referring to in verses 8 through 10?

1) Why does Paul bring up the issue of the law?

In verses 5 through 7 Paul makes mention of some who have strayed and turned aside to idle talk (see verses 5–6). These desire to be teachers of the law, though ignorant of what they claim is their expertise (see verse 7). In verse 8, a contrast is begun between the way those who have strayed use the law and the proper use of the law. This contrast is completed in verse 11. Why does Paul bring up the issue of the law? He does so to combat the wrong use of the law and set forth its right use. The law was being used unlawfully by some, and Paul aims to present its lawful use. (See Titus 3:9 for another instance of an unlawful use of the law.)

2) What is said about the law?

In verse 8 Paul says, "the law is good if one uses it lawfully." The law is both good and can be used lawfully. There is obviously a lawful and unlawful use of the law. Those described in verses 5 through 7 used the good law unlawfully, but Paul is going to show its lawful use. Commenting on that which "we know" about the law, New Testament scholar George Knight says:

> That which "we know" is "that the law is good" . . . The statement has striking similarities with several in Romans 7 (Rom. 7:14, 16 . . .). The point in 1 Tm. 1:8, as in Romans 7, is to affirm that the . . . [law] is intrinsically good because it is given by God (cf. Romans 2; 7:22; 8:4) and is not to be considered bad, though it can be mishandled, with bad results, as the . . . [law-teachers] have done.[34]

It is very clear that in this passage the law is viewed in its intrinsic goodness as it reveals proper, God-defined moral behavior.

3) To whom is Paul referring in verse 9 when he says, "the law is not made for a righteous person"?

Some understand "a righteous person" to refer to the justified, the saved, the Christian, without qualification. "This view acknowledges that the law functions to bring a person to Christ as a sinner but goes on to assert that a saved person is not to be concerned with or directed by the law."[35] This view is contradicted by many texts in Paul's writings, for instance Romans 7:14, 16, 22, 25, 13:8–10; and especially 2 Timothy 3:16–17, along with other texts in the New Testament (Matt. 5:17–18; James 2:8–11). It also does not fit the context. It is simply and emphatically not true that the law has no place in the life of the Christian.

What then does Paul mean? Knight offers the following explanation.

---

34. George W. Knight III, *The Pastoral Epistles: A Commentary on the Greek Text,* (Grand Rapids, MI: Wm. B. Eerdmans Publishing Company, 1992, re. 1996), 81.

35. Knight, *The Pastoral Epistles,* 80.

The meaning of . . . [righteous] here would seem to be determined in large measure by its place preceding and contrasting with a list of terms concerned with moral behavior. Therefore, the point of this section is to emphasize, against the would-be . . . [law-teachers], that the law is given to deal with moral questions and not for speculation. The would-be . . . [law-teachers] are not Judaizers like those of Galatians, since the PE [Pastoral Epistles] give no evidence of that, but rather those who deal with God's law from the perspective of myths, genealogies, and disputes about it (v. 4; see Tit. 3:9). Thus Paul is saying that the law is not given to apply in some mystical way to people who are already "righteous," i.e., those already seeking to conform to the law. It is, rather, given to deal with people who are specifically violating its sanctions and to warn them against their specific sins (as the list in vv. 9b–10 goes on to do).[36]

The Expositor's Greek Testament agrees with Knight's interpretation, when it says: ". . . [righteous] is used here in the popular sense, as in 'I came not to call the righteous.'"[37] The "righteous person" is anyone in *external* conformity to the law, whether Christian or non-Christian.[38] Patrick Fairbairn seems to agree, when he says:

By the latter expression [righteous] is to be understood, not one who in a worldly sense is just or upright (for the apostle is not here speaking of such), but who in the stricter sense is such,—one who, whether by nature or by grace, has the position and character of a righteous man. Why is the law not made for such? It can only be because he is of himself inclined to act in conformity with its requirements.[39]

These "righteous" ones are those who *conform* to the law. The word *righteous* is used elsewhere in the New Testament to

---

36. Knight, *Pastoral Epistles,* 83.
37. W. Robertson Nicoll, ed., *The Expositor's Greek Testament, Volume IV,* (Grand Rapids, MI: Wm. B. Eerdmans Publishing Company, re. 1988), 95.
38. This means that Christians may be in external and internal conformity to the law at the same time.
39. Patrick Fairbairn, *The Pastoral Epistles,* (Minneapolis, MN: Klock & Klock Christian Publishers, Inc., re. 1980), 87.

refer to non-Christians and Christians. For instance, Paul uses a form of this word in Philippians 3:6, when he says, ". . . concerning the righteousness which is in the law, blameless." Philippians 3:6 is Paul's own description of his relationship to the Mosaic Law before his conversion (see Phil. 3:9; Luke 1:5–6; and Acts 10:22). A person can be "righteous" and not a Christian.

In James 5:16 we read, "The effective, fervent prayer of a righteous man avails much." James 5:16 views Elijah as a believer, as "a righteous person" (see Matt. 25:37, 46; and Rom. 5:19). A person can be "righteous" and a Christian.

According to this understanding, Paul is not referring to the law in a *soteriological* sense, as it would point to Christ, but in an *ethical* sense, as it defines proper behavior for man. In the sense that the law defines proper behavior and rebukes those not in conformity to it, it is not for "a righteous person," for such a person is already conforming to it.[40] However, what about the person who is not conforming to the standards of the law? He is obviously not "a righteous person" in the sense intended by Paul. It is this person or persons that this use of the law is for.

This understanding of the passage makes conformity to the law the responsibility of believers and unbelievers alike. The law is the standard for proper conduct as defined by God for all mankind, Christian or non-Christian. This lawful use of the law points out sin and defines that conduct which "is contrary to sound doctrine, according to the glorious gospel."[41] Notice in verses 10 and 11 that living according to the sins listed in verses 9 and 10 "is contrary to sound doctrine,

---

40. Knight adds: "The 'righteous' are, then, those living in conformity to the requirements of the law by the work of Christ wrought by the Spirit in them (cf. Rom. 8:4 . . .). But Paul does not use 'righteous' here in an absolutistic way such that he himself would not have been inconsistent to refer to the law for the Christian (cf. Rom. 13:8–10), but in that less than absolute way which we see in Jesus—in a different situation and with a different nuance—but nonetheless in a nonabsolute way (Lk. 5:32: 'I have come to call not the righteous but sinners to repentance')." See Knight *The Pastoral Epistles*, 83. The nuance of Luke 5:32 is negative and the nuance of 1 Timothy 1:9 is positive.

41. See *Ibid*, 89–90 for a discussion on the prepositional phrase "according to the glorious gospel" which argues for the understanding taken above.

according to the glorious gospel." In other words, lawless living is antithetical to sound gospel doctrine.

If living according to the vices in 1 Timothy 1:9–10 is sinful living and "contrary to sound doctrine, according to the glorious gospel," then living in opposition to the vices is righteous living in accordance with "sound doctrine, according to the glorious gospel." In other words, for Christians, living antithetical to the vices in 1 Timothy 1:9–10 constitutes not an abrogation of the law, but a fulfillment of the law, which is "sound doctrine, according to the glorious gospel." This shows that the law is for the Christian to fulfill (see Rom. 8:4; 13:8, 10) and when he does so, he is living in conformity to "sound doctrine, according to the glorious gospel." "The sound doctrine demands that man *must* keep God's law."[42]

The gospel does not *replace* the law; it *upholds* the law. John Stott says:

> It is particularly noteworthy that sins which contravene the law (as breaches of the Ten Commandments) are also contrary to the sound doctrine of the gospel. So the moral standards of the gospel do not differ from the moral standards of the law. We must not therefore imagine that, because we have embraced the gospel, we may now repudiate the law![43]

Knight agrees:

> . . . the "sound teaching" [doctrine] of the Christian faith has the same ethical perspective as the law, and . . . that teaching also points out sins that are contrary to it. . . . By this Paul indicates that law and "sound teaching" [doctrine] are together in opposing these sins and therefore have a common ethical perspective.[44]

---

42. William Hendriksen, *New Testament Commentary, Thessalonians, Timothy and Titus*, (Grand Rapids, MI: Baker Book House, re. 1981), 71. The emphasis is Hendriksen's.

43. John Stott, *Guard the Truth*, (Downers Grove, IL: InterVarsity Press, 1996), 50.

44. Knight, *The Pastoral Epistles*, 88.

Living according to the list of vices in 1 Timothy 1:9–10 is sin for the Christian and non-Christian alike.[45]

4) What law is Paul referring to in verses 8 through 10? Some commentators believe Paul is referring to law in general and not the Mosaic Law. This view is inadequate. First, when Paul details for us the lawful use of the law, he clearly refers to commands contained in the Law of Moses. Second, "The ethical list in vv. 9–10 is similar to the Decalogue and the application of it in Exodus 21."[46] Third, in verses 5 through 7, where Paul brings up the would-be law-teachers, it seems clear that there is an assumed and well-known law. Fourth, in Titus 3:9 the law is mentioned, and again, in a way which simply assumes a well-known law. Fifth, it would be very difficult not to read these statements on the law in light of the rest of Paul's letters, which deal extensively with this very issue.

What law is Paul referring to? Consider the following observations. In verse 8 Paul uses an article before the word *law*. "But we know that *the* [emphasis added] law is good. . . ." This indicates that Paul is referring to an identifiable body of law.[47] It is clear from verses 9b and 10 that Paul had in mind at least the fifth through the ninth commandments of the Decalogue. Knight

---

45. William Hendriksen seems to concede this when he says, "The apostle now gives a summary of the law of the Ten Commandments. That summary shows clearly that there is no room for *anyone (least of all for the Ephesian errorists)* [emphasis Hendriksen's] to sit at ease in Zion. . . ." Hendriksen, *New Testament Commentary, Thessalonians, Timothy and Titus*, 67.

46. Knight, *The Pastoral Epistles*, 81.

47. The article, *the*, is not used before *law* in verse 9. However, it is somewhat common for Paul to not use an article after doing so previously in the context. The function of the article carries over from verse 8 to verse 9, which means that Paul is referring to the same law in both verses. See the comments by Murray below in the footnote (page 79) on Romans 2:14 and Henry Alford, *Alford's Greek Testament, Volume III*, (Grand Rapids, MI: Guardian Press, 1976), 306, where he says, ". . .not, 'a law' in general, as will be plain form the preceding remarks: nor does the omission of the article furnish any ground for such a rendering, in the presence of numerous instances where . . . [law], anarthrous [without the article], is undeniably 'the Law' of Moses." He then lists several instances and adds, "to say nothing of the very many examples after prepositions."

agrees, when he says, ". . . from 'strikers of father and mother' onward the order of the second part of the Decalogue is followed . . ."[48] It is also clear that Paul summarizes violations of the fifth through the ninth commandments with single words in the Greek text. Knight says, ". . . single words are used in the latter part of the list to refer to violators of a specific commandment. . . ."[49] The terms "murderers of fathers" and "murderers of mothers" are single word summaries of the fifth commandment in terms of its violation. The term "manslayers" is a single word summary of the sixth commandment in terms of its violation. The terms "fornicators" and "sodomites" are single word summaries of the seventh commandment in terms of its violation. The term "kidnappers" is a single word summary of the eighth commandment in terms of its violation. The terms "liars" and "perjurers" are single word summaries of the ninth commandment in terms of its violation.[50] Paul's list clearly reflects both the *content* and *order* of the second part of the Decalogue.

Our final observation concerning what law Paul is referring to is best put in the form of a question. What part of the Mosaic Law do the sins listed before verse 9b reflect? If the sins in 9b and 10 reflect both the *content* and *order* of the Decalogue, should we expect the sins in 9a to do so as well? In other words, since verses 9b and 10 reflect the *content* and *order* of the second part of the Decalogue, does verse 9a reflect the *content* and *order* of the first part?[51] Homer Kent says, ". . . the list of sins that appears

---

48. Knight, *The Pastoral Epistles*, 84.

49. *Ibid.* Two words refer to the fifth commandment. However, it is very clear from the words themselves that each points to the fifth commandment. "Murderers of fathers" refers to those who don't honor their father; "murderers of mothers" refers to those who don't honor their mother. In addition, two words refer to both the seventh commandment and the ninth commandment (see above).

50. See Knight, *The Pastoral Epistles,* 85–86, and J.H. Bernard, *Cambridge Greek Testament for Schools and Colleges, The Pastoral Epistles,* (Cambridge, England: At the University Press, 1899), 27–28, where this pattern is shown in more detail.

51. This is partially suggested by John MacArthur, author and general editor, *The MacArthur Study Bible,* (Nashville, TN: Word Publishing, 1997), 1860–1861, note on 1 Tim. 1:9. "These first 6 characteristics, expressed in

three couplets, delineate sins from the *first half* [emphasis added] of the Ten Commandments, which deal with a person's relationship to God." See also Geoffrey B. Wilson, *The Pastoral Epistles*, (Carlisle, PA: The Banner of Truth Trust, 1982), 24, where he says, "In a characteristic enumeration Paul sets forth the positive function of the law. The list follows the order of the Ten Commandments. The first three pairs cover offenses against God, while the vices mentioned are all violations of the second table of the law." *The MacArthur Study Bible* claims that 1 Timothy 1:9 contains three couplets. Assuming this to be the case and that by couplet one means a pair of synonyms separated by *and*, someone might want to argue that since there are three couplets above the terms that refer to those who violate the fifth commandment, then only three of the commandments of the first part of the Decalogue are referenced. This could be a way to exclude one of the first four commandments from the list. Michael Griffiths does this very thing, excluding the second command-ment. See Michael Griffiths, *Timothy and Titus*, (Grand Rapids, MI: Baker Books, 1996), 35–36. This seems very difficult for the following reasons. First, it is obvious that two terms in 1 Timothy 1:9b "murders of fathers" and "mur-ders of mothers," which both refer to the fifth commandment of the Decalogue and are separated by *and* do not function as a couplet, as defined above. A couplet, as defined above, contains two words that are synonymous. However, these terms, which represent the fifth commandment, are not synonymous. This specific two-term structure is necessary to reflect the two-fold nature of the fifth commandment. "Honor your *father* and your *mother*." No other com-mands of the Decalogue have compound objects. Second, Paul does not use couplets, as defined above, to refer to single commands of the Decalogue else-where. Third, there is good reason to believe that Paul is not using the rhetori-cal device of couplet, as defined above, in this passage at all. Both Blass and Debrunner and Robertson suggest that Paul is using two rhetorical devices called polysyndeton and asyndeton. Polysyndeton is a rhetorical devise which repeats the word *and* in a list of words. Asyndeton is a rhetorical devise which omits the word *and* in a list. Blass and Debrunner, say, "Asyndeton appears naturally in lengthy enumerations, if only for the sake of convenience; there is an inclination, however, to combine pairs in the interests of clarity . . . up to the point where this becomes burdensome (1 T 1:10). If a series is not strictly a summary but merely an enumeration, asyndeton may even be necessary." F. Blass and A. Debrunner, *A Greek Grammar of the New Testament and Other Early Christian Literature,* (Chicago, IL: The University of Chicago Press, 1961), 240. Elsewhere (230), Blass and Debrunner say that sometimes *and* may "form pairs which are asyndetic among themselves." Among the examples given are Acts 1:13 and 1 Timothy 1:9. Acts 1:13 in the Greek text illustrates this phenom-enon very clearly. Robertson says, "Perhaps, as Blass suggests, polysyndeton is sometimes necessary and devoid of any particular rhetorical effect, as in Lu. 14:21. . . . Sometimes the connective is used with part of the list (pairs) and not with the rest, for the sake of variety, as in 1 Tm. 1:9f." A.T. Robertson, *A Gram-mar of the Greek New Testament in the Light of Historical Research*, (Nashville,

in verses 9 and 10 seems clearly to follow the order of the Ten Commandments."[52] Fairbairn goes so far as to say:

> [L]aw so considered, unless the context plainly determines otherwise, always bears pointed reference to the decalogue; for this was the law in the more emphatic sense—the heart and essence of the whole economy of law; hence alone deposited in the ark of the covenant. And that this here also is more especially in the eye of the apostle, is evident from the different sorts of character presently after mentioned as intended to be checked and restrained by the law: they admit of being all ranged under the precepts of the two tables.[53]

Listen to Knight again.

> Once it is recognized that from "strikers of father and mother" onward the order of the second part of the Decalogue is followed, then the question naturally arises

---

TN: Broadman Press, 1934), 427. Fourth, a very plausible case can be made which shows that Paul reduces nine of the Ten Commandments, including the fourth, to single words in terms of their violation from this text (see the exposition above and especially the treatment of the word *profane* below). It must be granted that there are four pairs of terms in the Greek text of 1 Timothy 1:9 separated by *and*. The first pair functions as introductory and gives a two-fold description of who the law is for (see comments below); the second and third are single word summaries of the first through fourth commandments (see comments below); the fourth contains single word summaries of the fifth commandment. If one defines couplet as a pair of words separated by *and* though not necessarily synonymous, then I suppose we could call these pairs couplets.

52. Homer A. Kent, Jr., *The Pastoral Epistles,* (Chicago, IL: Moody Press, 1986), 82.

53. Fairbairn, *The Pastoral Epistles,* 87. Several commentators agree. See for instance, Walter Lock, *A Critical and Exegetical Commentary on the Pastoral Epistles, (ICC),* (Edinburgh, Scotland: T. & T. Clark, 1924, re. 1973), 12, and Alford, *Alford's Greek Testament, Volume III,* 306. J.H. Bernard says that the order of the Decalogue is followed from "*the* unholy and profane," but applies both of these terms to the third commandment exclusively. He says, "These lawless ones are now more exactly described, the order of the Decalogue being followed, and the extremest form of the violation of the Commandment being specified in each case." J.H. Bernard, *Cambridge Greek Testament for Schools and Colleges, The Pastoral Epistles,* 27.

whether the preceding part of the list in v. 9 corresponds to the earlier part of the Decalogue. An interesting correlation may well exist, especially if it is borne in mind that single words are used in the latter part of the list to refer to violators of a specific commandment, and therefore single words could also be used in the former part to characterize violators of the earlier commandments.[54]

Commenting on all of the vices in verses 9 and 10, Fairbairn says, "they admit of being all ranged under the precepts of the two tables."[55] He goes on to say:

> In regard to those for whom, he says, the law is made,—those, that is, who need the check and restraint of its discipline,—the apostle gives first a general description. . . . Then he branches out into particulars, the earlier portion of which have respect to offences against God, the latter to offences against one's fellowmen. . . .[56]

Alfred Plummer adds:

> In rehearsing the various kinds of sinners for who law exists, and who are found to be (he hints) among these false teachers, he goes roughly through the Decalogue. The four commandments of the First Table are indicated in general and comprehensive terms; the first five commandments of the Second Table are taken one by one, flagrant violators being specified in each case.[57]

---

54. Knight, *The Pastoral Epistles*, 84.

55. Fairbairn, *The Pastoral Epistles*, 87.

56. *Ibid*, 88. Fairbairn holds that the latter part of the list is dealing specifically with commands contained in the second part of the Decalogue, the former dealing generically and not referring to any specific command. Kent holds a similar view, where he says, "The first table of the Decalogue is covered in general terms by these three pairs of words." Kent, *The Pastoral Epistles*, 84. Kent seems to acknowledge that the three pairs do refer to each of the first four commandments and in order.

57. Alfred Plummer, *The Pastoral Epistles,* (New York, NY: Hodder & Stoughton, nd.), 45.

Let us take a closer look at verse 9 by going backward from Paul's reference to the fifth commandment at the end of the verse.[58] The first sin category mentioned by Paul going backward from "murderers of fathers and mothers" is the "profane." The noun form of *profane* is used of persons in the New Testament only twice, here in 1 Timothy 1:9 and in Hebrews 12:16. The verb form of *profane* is used of persons twice in the New Testament as well.[59] In Acts 24:6, it is used in the context of profaning the temple. In Matthew 12:5, it is used in the context of profaning the Sabbath. Concerning the verb form of the word *profane*, the *Theological Dictionary of the New Testament* says:

"To desecrate,": . . .
Common in the LXX[60], . . . thus . . . of the *holy day* [emphasis added] of God in Neh. 13:17f. . . . In the NT the only use is at Mt. 12:5 of the violation of the Sabbath and at Acts 24:6 of that of the temple, in both cases in the sense of the OT view of holiness. . . .[61]

One Greek-English lexicon indicates that the Septuagint uses this word to refer to desecrating or profaning the Sabbath in Nehemiah 13:17, Ezekiel 20:13, and Isaiah 56:2.[62] The LXX also uses "to profane" in Exodus 31:14; Isaiah 56:6; Ezekiel 20:16, 21, 24, 22:8, 38, all in the context of the Sabbath. The participial form of "to profane" is used in only three verses in the LXX: Isaiah 56:2, 6 and Ezekiel 23:39. Both Isaiah texts refer to

---

58. This approach is borrowed from Knight, *The Pastoral Epistles*, 84, from which I will quote extensively at this point.

59. The verb form describes objective action. The noun form describes subjective disposition.

60. LXX is the Roman numeral for seventy and refers to the Septuagint. The Septuagint is a Greek translation of the Old Testament with which Paul was very familiar.

61. Geoffrey W. Bromiley, translator, *Theological Dictionary of the New Testament*, (Grand Rapids, MI: Wm. B. Eerdmans Publishing Company, 1964, re. 1979), 605.

62. William F. Arndt, and F. Wilbur Gingrich, translators, *A Greek-English Lexicon of the New Testament and Other Early Christian Literature*, (Chicago, IL: The University of Chicago Press, 1957), 138.

profaning the Sabbath and the Ezekiel text to profaning the sanctuary. In the LXX of Ezekiel 22:26, the word *profane* is used three times in a context that includes breaking the Sabbath. Hiding their eyes from the Sabbath was one way Old Covenant priests could "profane" God. Notice that the Septuagint uses a form of the word *profane* in Isaiah 56:2 (see Isa. 56:6 as well) in the context of the Sabbath being defiled (verse 2) and kept (verse 4). This is especially instructive considering the fact that Isaiah's prophecy concerns the interadvental days of the New Covenant.[63] The word *profane* then refers to breaking the fourth commandment.[64]

This view is supported by several considerations. Paul was very familiar with the Septuagint. He was reducing other commands of the Decalogue to one word. He was following the *content* and *order* of other commands of the Decalogue. He was reducing other commands of the Decalogue to single words in a negative form.[65] Knight concludes, "Since the keynote of the

---

63. Isaiah's prophecy poses an insurmountable problem for New Covenant Theology's view of the Sabbath. New Covenant theologians identify the Sabbath, the fourth commandment of the Decalogue, as *the* sign of the Old Covenant and, therefore, as abrogated, in total, with the Old Covenant. This view seems to preclude any future, eschatological Sabbath, i.e., the Sabbath of Old Testament prophecy (Is. 56; 58; and Ezek. 44) without the reinstitution of the Old Covenant. Either the Old Covenant will be reinstituted (impossible according to New Covenant Theology), or the New Covenant has a Sabbath (also impossible according to New Covenant Theology). Since New Covenant Theology denies the former, then New Covenant Theology must affirm the latter, but cannot, due to identifying the Sabbath as *the* sign of the Old Covenant. If New Covenant theologians affirm that the New Covenant has a Sabbath, then non-premillennial New Covenant theologians must affirm a present millennial (i.e., interadvental) Sabbath, and premillennial New Covenant theologians must affirm a future millennial Sabbath in fulfillment of Old Testament prophecy. If the Sabbath is *the* sign of the Old Covenant, exclusively, what is it doing in a *New Covenant* prophecy?

64. Michael Griffiths applies the third pair of terms exclusively to the fourth commandment. See Griffiths, *Timothy and Titus*, 36. Kent applies the third pair of terms to the third and fourth commandments. See Kent, *The Pastoral Epistles*, 83–84.

65. It is of interest to note that the fourth commandment is considered *negatively* ("defiling"; "profaning" NASB) in Isaiah 56:2, 6 and *positively* ("keep")

sabbath is to keep it holy (. . . Ex. 20:8 . . .) and since Paul's list is in negative terms, the single term, . . . [profane], might well characterize those who profane that day, putting the command negatively in terms of its violation. . . ."[66] This sin is a violation of the fourth commandment of the Decalogue.

This understanding of 1 Timothy 1:9 provides the repetition of the fourth commandment of the Decalogue in the New Testament in a most instructive context. First, it comes in a context dealing with the Mosaic Law. Second, it comes in a context that includes other commands of the Decalogue. Third, it comes in a context that follows the *content* and *order* of the Decalogue. Fourth, it comes in a context where other commands of the Decalogue are reduced to single words in terms of their violation. Fifth, it comes in a context applicable to both believers and unbelievers.

This answers the objection often brought against the perpetuity of the fourth commandment, which says that since it is not repeated, it is not binding, and the objection that says that it was unique to Israel as God's Old Covenant nation. If the understanding of this text offered above is correct, then the fourth commandment is both *repeated* in the New Testament and *binding* on all men. This would mean that believers and unbelievers may be explicitly indicted for violating the essence of the fourth commandment after the Old Covenant has been replaced by the New Covenant. This would also mean that the Mosaic Law and the fourth commandment of the Decalogue both contain Moral Law.

in Isaiah 56:4. The Hebrew word *keep* in Isaiah 56:4 means to watch or preserve, whereas the Hebrew word for "keep it holy" in Exodus 20:8 means to set apart or consecrate. The opposite of defiling or profaning the Sabbath is keeping or preserving the Sabbath. Since Paul is reducing the commands of the Decalogue to single words in terms of their violation, he could well have the LXX version of Isaiah 56 in mind. Isaiah states the violation of the fourth commandment in a single word in terms of its violation and the LXX uses the very word Paul does. A similar phenomenon occurs in the LXX version of Ezekiel 44:23, 24. I owe this observation to Dr. Jim Renihan of the Institute for Reformed Baptist Studies, Westminster Theological Seminary, Escondido, California.

66. Knight, *The Pastoral Epistles*, 84.

The second sin category going backward from "murderers of fathers and mothers" mentioned by Paul is "*the* unholy." Knight says:

> Likewise, those who take the Lord's name in vain (Ex. 20:7) might well be designated negatively by a single term as those who are "unholy". . . . This understanding is strengthened if the language associated with this command has been influenced by the petition of the Lord's Prayer that the Lord's name be hallowed or regarded as holy (Mt. 6:9; Lk. 11:2).[67]

This sin is a violation of the third commandment of the Decalogue.

The third sin category going backward from "murderers of fathers and mothers" mentioned by Paul is "sinners." The Greek word for *sinner*

> is often used in the NT [New Testament] with the broad meaning "sinner," as it is in 1 Tim. 1:15. . . . At times, however, it is used in the NT more specifically of those who fail to keep the Mosaic law, particularly Gentiles, especially because of their idolatry. . . . This usage is found also in Paul in Gal. 2:15 (cf. on idolatry Rom. 2:22). Thus one who violates the prohibition of making and worshipping idols (Ex. 20:4–6) might well be designated a "sinner" in the specific sense (so Ex. 20:5 LXX . . .).[68]

This sin is a violation of the second commandment of the Decalogue.

The fourth sin category going backward from "murderers of fathers and mothers" mentioned by Paul is "*the* ungodly." "[T]he first commandment of the Decalogue (Exod. 20:3) prohibits

---

67. Knight, *The Pastoral Epistles*, 84.
68. Knight, *The Pastoral Epistles*, 84. As noted above by Knight, the Greek word for *sinner* is used in the second commandment of the Decalogue in the LXX. This is further evidence supporting the view that Paul had the LXX in mind while formulating certain aspects of this list. See *Ibid*, 87–88 for a discussion on Paul's partial dependence on the LXX while formulating this list of vices.

having other gods and abandoning God as the one and only true God. . . ."[69] The New Testament uses a positive form of the word Paul uses here in 1 Timothy 1:9, "ungodly", "of those who accepted the ethical monotheism of the OT [Old Testament] (see Acts 13:43, 50; 16:14; 17:4, 17; 18:7)"[70], though they were not even Christians. In other words, those in the texts just cited were not violating the first commandment, at least externally, and those in 1Timothy 1:9, "*the* ungodly," were. This sin is a violation of the first commandment of the Decalogue.

It seems quite clear that Paul follows both the *content* and the *order* of the Decalogue from the first through the ninth commandment in this list of sins, which are "contrary to sound doctrine, according to the glorious gospel." Knight concludes, and rightly so, "The order of the Decalogue seems, then, to give a satisfactory explanation of Paul's list from ["*the* ungodly"] onward."[71]

One question remains. What about the first two sins in Paul's list, "*the* lawless and insubordinate"? These first pair of terms function as a general introduction to the more specific list that follows. "These two terms bring into perspective those for whom the law is given, namely, those who need its discipline and restraint in their propensity for lawlessness and disobedience."[72]

Knight's concluding comments serve as a fitting end to our study of this crucial text.

> Paul has shown how the law may be used lawfully in accordance with its purpose as an ethical guide to warn against

---

69. Knight, *The Pastoral Epistles*, 84. As noted above by Knight, the Greek word for *sinner* is used in the second commandment of the Decalogue in the LXX. This is further evidence supporting the view that Paul had the LXX in mind while formulating certain aspects of this list. See *Ibid*, 87–88 for a discussion on Paul's partial dependence on the LXX while formulating this list of vices.

70. Knight, *The Pastoral Epistles,* 84.

71. *Ibid*. John Stott recently said, "This reconstruction is certainly ingenious and may be correct although it has to be declared unproved." Stott, *Guard the Truth*, 49. I have attempted to build upon Dr. Knight's work and prove its validity.

72. Knight, *The Pastoral Epistles*, 85.

sin. He has demonstrated this by presenting a list that shows that the Decalogue is so understood in the OT [Old Testament]. He has concluded by stating that this is also the ethical perspective of the truly healthy teaching based on the gospel, so that both it and a proper use of the law concur in terms of their concern for a righteous life and in their teaching against sin. Thus when the law is rightly applied as an ethical restraint against sin, it is in full accordance with the ethical norm given in the gospel as the standard for the redeemed life. A different use of the law, for example, in a mythological or genealogical application to the righteous, is thereby shown to be out of accord with the law's given purpose and the gospel and its teaching.[73]

It now becomes quite obvious what law Paul was referring to in 1 Timothy 1:8–11. He was referring to the heart of the law of the Old and New Covenants. He was referring to the basic, fundamental law of the Bible. He was referring to the law common to believer and unbeliever alike, the law whose work is written on the hearts of all men by creation. He was referring to the Decalogue in its function of revealing God-defined, ethical norms for all men.[74]

First Timothy 1:8–11 now becomes for us a vital text in the whole question surrounding the function of the Decalogue outside the Old Covenant as a unit. According to the exposition of this text, both Christians and non-Christians are held to an ethi-

---

73. Knight, *The Pastoral Epistles*, 91–92.

74. I realize that Paul does not refer to the tenth commandment of the Decalogue here. However, he does so in Romans 13:9 in a context clearly applying to Christians and in 1 Corinthians 6:10 in a context clearly applying to non-Christians. See *Ibid*, 87, for suggested reasons why Paul left out a reference to the tenth commandment. Alford offers the following explanation: "It is remarkable that he does not refer to that very commandment by which the law wrought on himself when he was alive without the law and sin was dead in him, viz. the tenth. Possibly this may be on account of its more spiritual nature, as he here wishes to bring out the grosser kinds of sin against which *the moral law* [emphasis added] is pointedly enacted. The subsequent clause however seems as if he had it in his mind, and on that account added a concluding general and inclusive description. . . ." *Alford's Greek Testament, Volume III*, 307.

cal standard that is reflected in the Decalogue. The utility of the Decalogue transcends the Old Covenant. Paul uses the Decalogue as the basic, fundamental law or body of ethical divinity applicable to *all* men. In Paul's thought, the Decalogue has more usefulness than simply as a temporary law governing the life of Israel under the Old Covenant. This point is supported by considering the fact that Paul was writing to Timothy who was ministering in Asia Minor (Ephesus), where Jews and Gentiles lived, at a time after the Old Covenant had been abolished and replaced by the New Covenant. First Timothy 1:8–11 is yet another New Testament text which assumes the abiding validity of the Decalogue outside of the Old Covenant as a unit. The very thing the New Testament clearly assumes, New Covenant Theology emphatically denies.

Challenge to New Covenant Theology

From the exposition of three New Testament texts, it has been shown that the Decalogue does function outside the Old Covenant as a unit. The Decalogue is the basic, fundamental law of the New Covenant and the basic fundamental law for all men, the Moral Law.

New Covenant theologians deny this crucial point. Strangely enough, even John Reisinger acknowledges that the Decalogue does have claims on unbelievers, though here he plainly contradicts himself. On the one hand, he claims the Old Covenant (Ten Commandments) was made with Israel at Sinai, given to Israel only, and had a historical beginning and a historical end (see above). On the other hand, he claims Christ fulfilled the Ten Commandments in the first century for Gentile Christians living in the twentieth century, nearly two thousand years after God's covenant with Israel, the Decalogue, in New Covenant thought, was abolished. Here are some exerts from his *Tablets of Stone*. Notice that he assumes to be true what he elsewhere declares impossible.

> The greater glory of the New Covenant is that *no obedience at all is required as the terms of being saved simply* because the very

terms of the Tablets of the Covenant have been *finally and fully met in the Person and work of Surety*, the Lord Jesus Christ.[75]

How can this be if the Decalogue was given to Israel as the first covenant? Are Gentiles somehow under the Old Covenant or are they under the Ten Commandments? If so, then the Decalogue functions outside of the Old Covenant. Summarizing Paul's understanding of the utility of the Decalogue today, Reisinger says:

> The Old Covenant written on the Tablets of Stone at Sinai have been "fulfilled" and done away. The claims of the Old Covenant have been met; it's [sic] curse has been endured and removed; and it's [sic] blessings have been secured by Christ and bestowed on His Church.[76]

This statement presupposes that Gentiles are responsible to keep the Decalogue. It implies that Gentiles are guilty before God for Sabbath breaking. These things cannot be, according to the major tenets of New Covenant Theology.

One last statement from Reisinger will suffice.

> It was the Tablets of Stone that blocked the way into the presence of God's presence, but now the terms of the covenant written on stone (Ten Commandments) have been fully met and we enter boldly into the Most Holy Place (Heb. 10:1–23).[77]

According to Reisinger, the Ten Commandments blocked the Gentiles from entrance to God's presence. How can this be? The only way is that the Gentiles must be responsible to keep the Decalogue. However, one of New Covenant Theology's ostensible *proofs* against the perpetuity of the Sabbath, the fourth commandment, is that Gentiles are nowhere indicted for breaking it. If the Ten Commandments blocked the Gentiles entrance into

---

75. Reisinger, *Tablets of Stone*, 51.
76. Reisinger, *Tablets of Stone,* 84.
77. *Ibid*, 85.

God's presence, then they must have been responsible to keep the Sabbath. It is inescapable: the Ten Commandments function outside the Old Covenant as a unit contrary to the claims of New Covenant Theology.

New Covenant Theology's insistence that the Old Covenant equals the Ten Commandments has been found wanting biblical support. New Covenant theologians are too quick to allow their understanding of one text, Exodus 34:27–28, to provide *the key* to the nature and function of the Ten Commandments throughout redemptive history. Neither the Old nor the New Testament supports such an assertion. Unfortunately, this unfounded presupposition precludes any function of the Ten Commandments other than *the* covenant with Israel in the minds of New Covenant Theology adherents.

In light of the exposition above, we may assert that the Decalogue functions three ways in Scripture: first as the basic, fundamental law of the Old Covenant; second, as the basic, fundamental law of the New Covenant; and third, as the basic, fundamental law common to all men, the Moral Law. In light of this, New Covenant theology's position on the identity of the Old Covenant and the function of the Ten Commandments in redemptive history emphatically must be rejected.

3

New Covenant Theology and the Abolition of the Old Covenant

The Issue at Stake

A third area of challenge for New Covenant Theology concerns its view of the abolition of the Old Covenant and the implications for New Covenant ethics. Hearty agreement must be given when New Covenant theologians argue for the abolition of the Old Covenant. This is clearly the teaching of the Old and New Testaments (see Jer. 31:31–32; 2 Cor. 3; Gal. 3, 4; Eph. 2:14–15; Heb. 8–10). The whole Law of Moses, *as it functioned under the Old Covenant*, has been abolished, including the Ten Commandments. Not one jot or tittle of the Law of Moses functions *as Old Covenant law* anymore, and to act as if it does constitutes redemptive-historical retreat and neo-Judaizing. However, to acknowledge that the Law of Moses no longer functions *as Old Covenant law* is not to accept that it no longer functions; it simply no longer functions *as Old Covenant law*. This can be seen by the fact that the New Testament teaches *both* the abrogation of the law of the Old Covenant *and* its abiding moral validity under the New Covenant. Two important texts illustrate this phenomenon very clearly: Matthew 5:17–20 and Ephesians 2:14–15.

Exposition of Matthew 5:17–20

In Matthew 5:17–20 we read:

> Do not think that I came to destroy the Law or the Prophets. I did not come to destroy but to fulfill. For assuredly, I say to

you, till heaven and earth pass away, one jot or one tittle will by no means pass from the law till all is fulfilled. Whoever therefore breaks one of the least of these commandments, and teaches men so, shall be called least in the kingdom of heaven; but whoever does and teaches *them*, he shall be called great in the kingdom of heaven. For I say to you, that unless your righteousness exceeds *the righteousness* of the Pharisees, you will by no means enter the kingdom of heaven.

A common understanding of this text goes like this: Jesus is saying that He will make the law null and void for His people and is declaring that they will have nothing to do with the Old Testament law of God because He will fulfill or complete it for them. This understanding often pits law and grace against each other, as if law keeping, or works, saved Old Testament saints; and faith, or grace, saves New Testament saints. Those who hold this view, or something similar to it, often put a wide gulf between Old Testament and New Testament ethics. The Old Testament becomes a book of the past with little relevance for the present. Those of this persuasion often say, "If not repeated in the New, the Old we will not do." Or, "We are not under the Law of Moses, but under the law of Christ," as if Moses and Christ are sworn enemies. This view has many problems.

First, this view cannot stand up against the context. In verse 17, the phrase "the Law or the Prophets" refer to the whole Old Testament. In John 15:25 the word *law* refers to the Psalms. In Romans 3:21 Paul uses the phrase "the Law and the Prophets." In 1 Corinthians 14:21 "the law" refers to Isaiah 28:11–12. In Galatians 4:21–31 "the law" includes portions of the book of Genesis (see especially verses 21 and 22). All of this shows that the word *law* in the New Testament may refer to the Law of Moses exclusively or to the whole Old Testament. In verse 18a, the phrase "till heaven and earth pass away," refers to the *duration* of the whole Old Testament's authority.[1] In other words, the

---

1. See Luke 20:34–35. This furnishes proof that heaven and earth have not passed away and that the age to come is yet future, both from Christ's vantage point and ours, because Christians still die, marry, and are given in marriage.

whole Old Testament is authoritative until the age to come. In verse 18b, the phrase, "one jot or one tittle," refers to the *extent* of the Old Testament's authority. This text teaches that the whole Old Testament is authoritative between the two advents of Christ, down to its minute detail. According to Matthew 5:17–18, the "Law and the Prophets" (the whole Old Testament) have their place under the administration of Christ in the New Covenant.

Second, this view often assumes a theory of the postponement of the kingdom of Christ that is explicitly disproved by the rest of the New Testament (see Acts 20:25 and Col. 1:13). Christ's statement concerning "the Law and the Prophets" applies to His Kingdom, which was inaugurated at His first coming and into which all Christians have been placed.

Third, this view cannot adequately deal with the pro-law statements of the New Testament (see Rom. 3:31; 7:22, 25; 8:4; 13:8–10; 1 Cor. 9:9; 14:34; and Eph. 6:1–3, which all clearly refer to the law of the Old Testament). If Christ's people are to have nothing to do with the law of the Old Testament, how do we understand these and other statements of the New Testament?

Fourth, this view cannot justify capital punishment as a duty of the civil magistrate. It can justify the presence of civil government, but it cannot give it the grave responsibility of taking life for life unless it breaks its own rules and makes binding under the New Testament something not explicitly repeated by the New Testament.

Fifth, this view cannot adequately explain 2 Timothy 3:16. In 2 Timothy 3:16–17, we read: "All Scripture is given by inspiration of God, and is profitable for doctrine, for reproof, for correction, for instruction in righteousness, that the man of God may be complete, thoroughly equipped for every good work." Scripture, in the context of this verse, refers primarily to the Old Testament, or as Paul says in verse 15, "the Holy Scriptures." Paul says, "All Scripture [the Old Testament] . . . is profitable for doctrine, for reproof, for correction, for instruction in *righteousness*," [emphasis added] and is such for a minister of the New Covenant. The Holy Scriptures are said to be both "able to make you wise unto salvation through faith which is in Christ

Jesus" and "profitable for . . . instruction in righteousness" (verse 17). It is the whole of Holy Scripture that Paul is referring to, not merely selected parts that are repeated in the New Testament by Christ and His apostles. This passage teaches us that the whole Old Testament is inspired of God and still profitable for men in Christian ministry under the New Covenant.

If this view of Matthew 5:17–20 is incorrect, what view of this text does justice to the text, the context, and the rest of the New Testament? Consider the following observations as an attempt to give a more plausible understanding of this vital text.[2]

First, notice the antithetical relationship between the concepts of "destroying" and "fulfilling" in verse 17. Christ did not come to obliterate the law, but to fulfill the law. This obviously means that "the Law or the Prophets" are not done away with [destroyed] as authoritative ethical directives for Christ's people.

Second, notice the scope of "the Law or the Prophets." As noted above, this refers to the whole Old Testament. The whole Old Testament has a place under Christ's lordship until His Second Coming. Both the *extent* and *duration* of Old Testament authority are spoken of here as argued above.

Third, observe the meaning of the word *fulfill*. What does Christ mean by this term? Some have tried to define this word to mean "confirm." They would have it mean that Christ came to confirm the validity of the Old Testament as it stands, though with some alterations. A more contextual understanding of this word allows for Matthew's use of it previously to help us with its definition and use in this context. For instance, in Matthew 2:14–15, we read: "When he arose, he took the young Child and His mother by night and departed for Egypt, and was there until the death of Herod, that it might be *fulfilled* which was spoken by the Lord through the prophet, saying, 'Out of Egypt I called my Son.'" Here the concept of fulfillment refers to the eschatological realization and application of an Old Testament text. Although

---

2. Much of my exposition of Matthew 5:17–20 is dependent upon D. A. Carson in Frank E. Gaebelein, General Editor, *The Expositor's Bible Commentary, Volume 8,* (Grand Rapids, MI: The Zondervan Corporation, 1984), 140–147. My application of the text differs, however.

no ethical dimension is involved in this case, the principle is illustrated nonetheless. What Christ does to the Law and the Prophets, the whole Old Testament, is to bring them to redemptive-historical maturity. Christ came to bring the Old Testament to an advanced stage of eschatological realization and application. Christ is fulfilling the law and will do so until heaven and earth pass away when He comes again and ushers in the age to come in its fullness and glory.[3]

What Jesus is saying is that the Old Testament is still binding upon His people, *but not in the same way it used to be.* The Old Testament is still authoritative as far as our sanctification goes, *but the coming and death of Christ and the inauguration of the New Covenant now condition its application.* New Testament scholar Vern Poythress agrees, when he says, "All the commandments of the law are binding on Christians . . ., but the way in which they are binding is determined by the authority of Christ and the fulfillment that takes place in His work."[4]

The rest of the New Testament confirms this thesis as established from Matthew 5:17–20. The New Testament is very clear that the law of the Old Testament is still authoritatively binding on the Church, though not always in the same way that it was as originally given (see Rom. 15:4; 1 Cor. 9:9; Deut. 25:4; 1 Cor. 10:1–13; 1 Tim. 5:17–18; Eph. 6:1–3; and 2 Tim. 3:16). Casting aside all the difficult questions that arise concerning the specific application of this thesis, it cannot be doubted that the rest of the New Testament clearly confirms it. The law of God, even the whole Old Testament, has its place under Christ, finding its realization in Him and its modified application in His kingdom. If the whole Old Testament is still binding, then certainly all its parts are as well.

---

3. See Romans 8:4 and 13:8, 10, where Christians, like their Savior, fulfill the law. Christ's fulfilling of the law does not set it aside and neither does the Christian's. When heaven and earth pass away, all the jots and tittles of the law shall pass away, and then all will be fulfilled.

4. Vern S. Poythress, *The Shadow of Christ in the Law of Moses*, (Phillipsburg, NJ: P&R Publishing, 1991), 268.

To sum up, Matthew 5:17–20 teaches us that the whole Old Testament, the Law and the Prophets, is assumed under the lordship of Christ and ethically binding until the eternal state comes in consummate glory. The meaning of the word *fulfill* in Matthew 5:17 in its Matthean context is vital. A contextual understanding of this word allows for Matthew's use of it previously to help us with its definition and use in this context. The Matthean concept of fulfillment refers to the eschatological realization and application of the Old Testament. What Christ does to the Old Testament is to bring it to redemptive-historical maturity. Christ came to bring the Old Testament to an advanced stage of eschatological realization and application. Christ is fulfilling the law and will do so until heaven and earth pass away, when He comes again and ushers in the age to come in its fullness and glory.

Exposition of Ephesians 2:14–16
In Ephesians 2:14–16 we read:

> For He Himself is our peace, who has made both one, and has broken down the middle wall of separation, having abolished in His flesh the enmity, that is, the law of commandments contained in ordinances, so as to create in Himself one new man from the two, thus making peace, and that He might reconcile them both to God in one body through the cross, thereby putting to death the enmity.

Two introductory observations from the context will help us focus in on the crucial verses of this passage (verses 14b and 15). First, in verses 11–13 of chapter two, Paul describes for us the former state of the Gentile Ephesians. Second, in verses 14–22 of chapter two, he describes for us the present unity of Jew and Gentile in the Church. It is clear from verses 15 and 16 that the death of Christ has produced this peace between Jew and Gentile and sinners and God.

With these contextual observations before us, it is a good time to ask a twofold question, which the text answers: What is "the middle wall of separation" of verse 14b and "the law of commandments *contained* in ordinances" of verse 15? Some commentators try to make this wall of separation the wall at the temple in Jerusalem, which kept Gentiles in the outer court and from the full privilege of temple worship. Others take it to mean the veil or curtain that separated the Holy Place from the Holy of Holies. Still, others take it to mean the racial enmity that existed between Jew and Gentile.

A modified view of the last position seems to do full justice to the context. Let us explore this. Paul seems to be saying, "Christ breaks down the middle wall of separation by invalidating that which was, in part, the promoter of the personal division between Jew and Gentile." What promoted the personal division between Jew and Gentile? It was their sinful hearts *and* the middle wall of separation. John Eadie, commenting on the wall between Jew and Gentile, says, "Any social usage, national peculiarity, or religious exclusiveness, which hedges round one race and shuts out all others from its fellowship, may be called a 'middle wall of partition [separation];' and such was the Mosaic law."[5] In other words, the middle wall of separation was the law of the Old Covenant.

Verse 15 goes on to verify this understanding by further explaining what Christ did to this wall. His death abolished or invalidated "the middle wall of separation," which is "the law of commandments *contained* in ordinances." These two concepts refer to the Old or Mosaic Covenant. It is very clear from this passage and other explicit statements of the New Testament that the Old Covenant and its law, *as Old Covenant law*, has been annulled by Christ's death. Though the law of the Old Covenant still exists and is *called* law, it no longer *functions* as the law of the Old Covenant, because the Old Covenant has been replaced by the New Covenant.

Paul Views the Old Covenant Law as Both Annulled and Binding
Now this in no way means that Paul is an Antinomian.[6] R.C. Sproul comments, "There is, in every generation, a constant threat to the church from a heresy called Antinomianism. The

---

5. Eadie, *Ephesians*, 173.
6. *Antinomian* literally means "against law."

Antinomian heresy is the view that the law of God revealed in the Old Testament has nothing to do with the New Testament church. . . ."[7] In saying that Christ's death annulled the Law of Moses, what is meant is that He annulled it *as Old Covenant law*. The Old Covenant has been replaced by the New Covenant. The Law of Moses no longer functions *as it once used to*; but this is not to say that it no longer functions.

This can be illustrated from Paul himself. He quotes part of the heart of the law of the Old Covenant, the Ten Commandments, in 6:2–3 of this very book of Ephesians. Hence, annulling the law of the Old Covenant does not mean it is in no way binding on the Christian. The New Testament clearly abrogates the whole Old Covenant, including the Decalogue, as it functioned within the Old Covenant, and yet borrows from its documents as the basis for New Covenant ethics (see for instance 1 Cor. 9:9–10; 14:34;[8] 2 Cor. 13:1; Eph. 6:2–3, and many other texts).

It may be helpful at this time to consider the two ways the New Testament views the Old Covenant.[9] First, the New Testament views the Old Covenant as a temporary covenant pointing forward to Christ, abolished by Christ, and replaced by the New Covenant (see Gal. 3:10–25 and Heb. 7:18–19; 8:1–7; 10:1). Second, the New Testament views the Old Covenant as a permanent revelation of binding moral principle (see Matt. 5:17–18; Rom. 3:19–20, 31; 7:12, 14; 13:8–10; 1 Cor. 9:9–10, and the all-inclusive 2 Tim. 3:16).

In sum, Ephesians 2:14–16 speaks of the abrogation of the Old Covenant as a covenant with ancient Israel. Again, the Law of Moses no longer functions as it once used to, but this is not to say that it no longer functions. It now functions as a part of New

---

7. R.C. Sproul, *Ephesians*, (Fearn Ross–shire, Scotland: Christian Focus Publications, 1994), 66.

8. This is not a quotation of Old Covenant law, but an obvious reference to the present moral obligation of women in the context of the Church, based on the overall teaching of Old Covenant law.

9. I am indebted to Pastor Sam Waldron of the Reformed Baptist Church of Grand Rapids, Michigan for this insight. See his unpublished *Lectures on the Lord's Day,* 11, which is available from Truth for Eternity Ministries, 3181 Bradford NE, Grand Rapids, MI 49505.

Covenant law (Matt. 5:17–20; 2 Tim. 3:16–17). Ephesians 2:14–16, and other New Testament texts, speak of the abrogation of the Old Covenant as a covenant with ancient Israel, but in no way makes the law of the Old Covenant as New Covenant law obsolete. The law of the Old Covenant is simply assumed into New Covenant law and applied as such by the New Testament. It must be granted that the redemptive-historical change brought on by Christ's death and the inauguration of the New Covenant causes the application of the law to differ, but this is not to say that the law is canceled in all respects. The law is the same; its application is modified to fit the conditions brought on by the death of Christ and the inauguration of the New Covenant.

Challenge to New Covenant Theology

New Covenant theologians give the appearance of not allowing the whole Old Testament to inform the content of New Covenant ethics. For instance, Zaspel says:

> It is the Mosaic code as a whole and in all its parts that has passed away, and the apostolic declarations to that end must therefore be seen to embrace even the Decalogue. . . . We would rather expect that for new covenant believers divine law would be codified in the new covenant.[10]

The error here is in not recognizing that, though the Old Covenant has been abrogated, the law of the Old Covenant now functions as part of New Covenant law. Simply put, the Christian ethic involves the whole Bible. The abrogation of the Old Covenant does not cancel the utility of the Old Testament.

---

10. Zaspel, "Divine Law," 155.

4

New Covenant Theology and the Sermon on the Mount

The Issue at Stake

A fourth area of challenge for New Covenant Theology concerns its understanding of the Sermon on the Mount. The Sermon on the Mount, found in Matthew 5–7, is one of the most precious portions of the Word of God. In it, the Lord Jesus expounds and applies part of the Moral Law of God.

The issue at stake with respect to New Covenant Theology concerns the statement, "But I say to you." This statement is used six times by the Lord Jesus in this sermon. According to New Covenant Theology, it is used to contrast Christ's teaching with the Law of Moses.[1] Christ is seen as "giving the Church a new canon of moral conduct."[2] Representative of this type of thinking are the following statements from Reisinger's *Christ, Lord and Lawgiver Over the Church.*

Christ did say, and say most clearly, that His law is *infinitely higher and more spiritual than anything Moses ever wrote.*

---

1. John Reisinger does acknowledge that Christ is correcting the distortions of the Pharisees in Matthew 5:43–44 (see Reisinger, *But I Say Unto You*, 53). However, this does not dismiss the radical statements he makes elsewhere concerning the function of the statement, "But I say to you," as contrastive with Moses. It seems much simpler to understand the statement to mean the same thing throughout the passage than to change its meaning.

2. Reisinger, *But I Say Unto You*, 2. This is put in the form of a question on page two and answered in the affirmative in the rest of the book as will be seen below.

Contrasting the Sermon on the Mount with the Tablets of Stone is like comparing the sun to a candle. Making the Sermon on the Mount to be only the *true interpretation of Moses* is to effectively deny Christ is a lawgiver and make him to be merely a *rubber stamp* of Moses.[3]

How we understand the "but I say unto you" contrasts in the Sermon on the Mount reveals our true attitude to the unique Lordship of Christ in His role of Lawgiver. Is Christ, in the Sermon on the Mount and the Epistles, giving us a higher standard of holiness than Moses ever gave or is He merely giving us the official spiritual explanation of what Moses actually meant in the law?[4]

Is Moses the final and full Lawgiver and Christ merely the true interpreter and enforcer of Moses, or is Christ the new Lawgiver Who supersedes and replaces Moses with higher laws? It is one or the other![5]

In chapter three of *But I Say Unto You,* entitled "New Lawgiver or Master of Logic", Reisinger says of Matthew 5:27–28, "It seems clear that the texts are showing that Christ was giving new and higher truth. . . . He [the Holy Spirit] will point every believer to the Cross and not to a sword, and this will move their hearts to love and obey My [Christ's] *new (objective) laws!*"[6] "The correct way to approach Mt. 5:27 is *just let it mean exactly what it says.* Let it really contrast the difference between rule under covenant law and rule under grace. . . ."[7] These types of statements could be multiplied.

Exposition of Matthew 5:27–28

Is Christ *giving the Church a new canon of moral conduct in Matthew chapter five*? Is Christ giving us a law *infinitely higher*

---

3. Reisinger, *Christ, Lord and Lawgiver . . .,* 13–14. These statements are fraught with unsubstantiated presuppositions, which will become more obvious below.

4. *Ibid,* 14.

5. *Ibid,* 16.

6. Reisinger, *But I Say Unto You,* 21.

7. *Ibid,* 22.

and more spiritual than anything Moses ever wrote? Is the Sermon
on the Mount *a contrast of the difference between rule under covenant law and rule under grace?* According to New Covenant
Theology, the "But I say to you" statements of the Sermon on
the Mount indicate to us that Christ is about to reveal new and
higher truth, which contrasts the law of Moses. But to "contrast" different things means "[t]o set in opposition in order to
show or emphasize differences."[8] Is Christ setting His new laws
in opposition to the Law of Moses in order to show and emphasize the differences between them? If so, then we would expect
Christ's laws to be found in the Sermon on the Mount and the
epistles, but *not* in the Law of Moses or the rest of the Old Testament. Otherwise, Christ's law would not be in opposition to the
Law of Moses. This we do not find. This is demonstrated merely
by an examination of Matthew 5:27–28 and its relationship to
the seventh commandment.

In Matthew 5:27–28, we read, "You have heard that it was
said, 'You shall not commit adultery.' But I say to you that whoever looks at a woman to lust for her has already committed
adultery with her in his heart." According to New Covenant
Theology, Christ is transcending the Law of Moses concerning
adultery. Under this approach, He is contrasting the seventh
commandment with verse 28. The "But I say to you" statement is Christ's indicator that what He is about to say is *new*
and *more spiritual than anything Moses ever wrote.* It is a sign to
the original audience and all audiences since that He is about
to set His law in opposition to Moses in order to show and
emphasize differences. In the words of Reisinger, "'Thou shalt
not commit adultery' has a higher and deeper meaning when
applied by Christ under the New Covenant than it could have
ever had when merely written on stone."[9] He continues, "The
correct way to approach Mt. 5:27 is *just let it mean exactly what*

---

8. William Morris, editor, *The American Heritage Dictionary of the English Language,* (New York, NY: American Heritage Publishing Co., Inc.,
1969), 290.
9. Reisinger, *But I Say Unto You,* 21–22.

it says. Let it really contrast the difference between rule under covenant law and rule under grace. . . ."[10]

If the New Covenant Theology formula is correct, we would have to conclude that Moses never explicitly or implicitly taught that adultery was more than an external, physical act. If New Covenant Theology is right, we would have to say that Moses intended only external, physical adultery by the seventh commandment and that the seventh commandment does not forbid the internal, heart adultery of Matthew 5:28. Indeed, we would have to say that no Old Testament text prohibited heart adultery, since what Christ is revealing is new. Yet the Law of Moses, in Exodus 20:17, the tenth commandment, clearly forbids heart adultery. "Thou shalt not covet . . . your neighbors wife. . . ."[11] The Proverbs as well clearly forbid heart adultery. Concerning the adulterous woman, Proverbs 7:25 says, "Do not let your heart turn aside to her ways. . . ." These are clear prohibitions against heart adultery! Matthew 5:28 is not new and contrastive in light of these texts. The Old Testament teaches the same thing. Therefore, the following questions need to be answered by adherents of New Covenant Theology: Did an Old Covenant man honor God by committing lust, the type of heart adultery forbidden by Matthew 5:28? Does the Bible wait until Matthew 5:28 to reveal the evil of lusting after women in the heart? The clear answer of Scripture to both these questions is "No!"

In sum, in forbidding lust, it is much easier and simpler to hold that Christ is stating *explicitly* what was already contained *implicitly* in the seventh commandment. He is not instituting a contrastive and new law in Matthew 5:28. Instead, He is correcting the faulty exegesis of the day. As John MacArthur rightly comments, "Jesus made no alteration to the true meaning of the law. He was merely explaining and affirming the law's true

---

10. Reisinger, *But I Say Unto You*, 22.

11. Granted, the tenth commandment does not use the same words as Matthew 5:28. However, one would be hard-pressed not to acknowledge a prohibition against heart adultery implied by the tenth commandment.

meaning."[12] Christ is saying that the heart adultery envisioned in Matthew 5:28 is the very same adultery forbidden by the seventh commandment and referenced by Him in Matthew 5:27. Therefore, using the Sermon on the Mount as an example · of Christ establishing a contrastive neo-ethic for the New Covenant simply will not work.

Challenge to New Covenant Theology

As this illustration alone reveals, New Covenant Theology makes some claims that are impossible to reconcile with the rest of Scripture. For example, Reisinger says, "Christ did say, and say most clearly, that His law is *infinitely higher and more spiritual than anything Moses ever wrote.*"[13] However, saying that Christ's law is *infinitely higher and more spiritual than anything Moses ever wrote* contradicts the fact that the law Christ expounded in the Sermon on the Mount and revealed in the epistles through His apostles includes portions of the very things Moses wrote, and sometimes without qualification. For instance, Paul quotes the Decalogue in Romans 13:9 without any New Covenant contrastive qualifications. Paul, then, appears to have no problem quoting the Decalogue and leaving it at that.

The bottom line is that the New Covenant Theology position on the Sermon on the Mount is untenable. Other portions of the Old Testament forbid what Christ forbids in Matthew 5:28, though in different words. Therefore, heart adultery is neither a new law nor contrastive with previous revelation. If it were new, then the Old Testament would not teach the same thing. If it were contrastive, then there would be striking dissimilarities between it and previous revelation. Hence, the New Covenant Theology understanding of the statement, "But I say to you," must be rejected and replaced with another understanding.

There is, of course, a better way to view Jesus' words, "But I say to you," in Matthew 5. Jesus *is* indeed introducing a contrast, but not between the Law of Moses and the Law of Christ.

---

12. MacArthur, *The MacArthur Study Bible*, 1402, note on Mt. 5:38.
13. Reisinger, *Christ, Lord and Lawgiver,* 13.

Rather, the contrast is between a true understanding of the Law
of Moses and the false understanding evidenced in the hypoc-
risy of the scribes and Pharisees. Matthew chapter six makes
very clear that Christ is contrasting true righteousness with hy-
pocrisy, not the Law of Moses. He instructs his disciples on the
correct way to give, pray, and fast, as contrasted with the Phari-
saical approaches to giving, prayer, and fasting. In Matthew
23:23–25, as well, Christ exposes the externalism of the scribes
and Pharisees much as He does in the Sermon on the Mount.
Thus, Christ is not altering the Law of Moses in the Sermon on
the Mount, but rightly applying it, unlike the scribes and Pharisees who were hypocrites. They distorted the Law of Moses by
settling for externalism. This was never God's intention in the
Law of Moses and the Old Covenant, as numerous Old Testament passages indicate (Exod. 25:2; Lev. 19:18; Deut. 6:5; 8:2;
10:12–13; 11:13, 18; and many Psalms).

5

New Covenant Theology and the Identity of the Moral Law[1]

The Issue at Stake

A fifth area of challenge for New Covenant Theology concerns the identity of the Moral Law, the law common to all men. Some New Covenant theologians appear to argue for the content of the Moral Law in this fashion: Since sins against nine of the Ten Commandments were punished by God prior to the promulgation of the Decalogue via Moses, and since those same nine commandments are repeated in the New Testament, then these nine commandments represent Moral Law. For instance, Fred Zaspel says:

> Important also is the recognition that this law of God in men's hearts from creation onward is nearly identical with the Decalogue, which came by Moses. Other than the fourth command (Sabbath) virtually all of the "Ten Words" were in force well before Moses. . . . The great bulk of the Decalogue, then, is clearly but a formal codification of the law of God that was (and is) in man's heart naturally.[2]

Likewise, John Reisinger says:

---

1. New Covenant theologians prefer the phrase "moral laws" instead of "the Moral Law." It will become evident that this is an unnecessary novelty or neologism—a new word or phrase.
2. Zaspel, "Divine Law," 148.

> Nine of the Ten Commandments were known by men and punished by God long before and after God gave them to Israel as a covenant at Sinai. Every specific duty commanded in the Ten Commandments *except the fourth, or Sabbath, was punished before Mt. Sinai, and likewise, every commandment except the fourth, is repeated in the NT Scriptures.*[3]

There is much to admire in this attempt to define what law of God is common to all men, the Moral Law. Romans 2:14–15 is used by some New Covenant theologians as the exegetical basis for this, and rightly so. However, there is at least one difficulty with this equation. Upon what exegesis can one get the rules for defining the Moral Law as those transgressed commandments of the Decalogue punished by God prior to the giving of the Tablets of Stone and repeated in the New Testament? It seems that this approach ends up arguing from the silence of the Bible and not its explicit teaching. Could other sins have been committed, though not mentioned during the time before the promulgation of the Decalogue, which would constitute a breach of the Moral Law? Silence proves silence; it does not define the Moral Law for us.

Exposition of Romans 2:14–15

Let us take a closer look at Romans 2:14–15 and try to identify the Moral Law, the law common to all men. In Romans 2:14–15, we read:

> for when Gentiles, who do not have the law, by nature do the things in the law, these although not having the law, are a law to themselves, who show the work of the law written in their hearts, their conscience also bearing witness, and between themselves *their* thoughts accusing or else excusing *them.*

Before commenting on these crucial verses, it is important to understand the context in which they occur. These verses come in the broader section, which begins in verse 12 and ends

---

3. Reisinger, *Tablets of Stone*, 79–80.

in verse 16. In verse 12, Paul's concern is to defend the justice of God in the condemnation of Gentiles without law. In verses 14 and 15, he gives his defense. Focusing in on verses 14 and 15, three questions confront us. What is the law possessed by the Jews in this context? Do Gentiles without special revelation possess law? What law do Gentiles without special revelation possess?

1) What is the law possessed by the Jews in this context?

The first reference to the law in verse 14 obviously refers to the law possessed by the Jews. This is clearly the law the Jews possessed via special revelation, Holy Scripture. This law is mentioned at the end of verse 12, in verses 13 and 14, and in several places in verses 17–27. In verses 21 and 22 reference is made to commands contained in the Decalogue. Paul therefore gives the impression that what he means by the law the Jews possessed is the basic, fundamental law of the Old Covenant, the Decalogue. Elsewhere in Romans, Paul refers to the law of the Old Covenant and immediately quotes parts of the Decalogue (see Rom. 13:8–10).

Some might want to say that the law of the Jews being referred to by Paul is either the whole Old Testament or the whole Law of Moses (torah), which includes the moral, ceremonial, and civil law of the Old Covenant. This would mean that, by way of general revelation, through creation, God writes Old Covenant ceremonial and civil laws on the hearts of all men, an untenable proposition. Ceremonial law is revealed after the fall into sin as part of special revelation. It is not general revelation. It presupposes the entrance of sin and is aimed at repairing the damage done by sin. No, the law referred to here by Paul is more basic and fundamental than ceremonial law. The law of the Gentiles referred to in this context is a law based on creation, not sin or even redemption. Therefore, the law that the Gentiles possess via general revelation cannot refer to the Old Testament as a whole or the Law of Moses as a whole. It must be referring to law that is basic and fundamental to man's status as creature and image bearer of God. It is a law all men possess by nature, because all men are created, and a law contained somewhere within the whole body of special revelation given to the Jews in the Old Testament. H.C.G. Moule agrees.

> Manifestly "*the* Law" in this passage means not the ceremonial law of Israel, but the revealed moral law given to Israel, above all in the Decalogue. This appears from the language of ver. 15, which would be meaningless if the reference were to special ordinances of worship. The Gentiles could not "shew the work of" *that* kind of "law written in their hearts"; what they shewed was, as we have explained, a "work" related to the revealed claims of God . . . on the will and life.[4]

2) Do Gentiles without special revelation possess law?

It is clear that the Gentiles did not possess the *externally* written law of the Jews as an *externally* written law; they did not possess the Old Testament. Does this mean that the Gentiles had no law? Scripture is very clear that if there is no law, there cannot be sin (see Rom. 4:15; 5:12–14; and 1 John 3:4). Surely Paul could not be saying the Gentiles did not possess law altogether. On the contrary, the Gentiles did possess law, but did not, and could not, live up to it and were thus indicted in Romans 1.

The law that the Gentiles did not possess was the *externally revealed* law of the Old Testament, as an *externally written* law. However, this in no way implies they did not possess law. Paul is very clear that they did. He proves this by asserting in verses 14 and 15 that ". . . when Gentiles, who do not have the law [the law in context refers to the *externally revealed* law of the Jews contained in the Old Testament], by nature do the things in the law [the *externally revealed* law of the Jews contained in the Old Testament], these, although not having the law [the *externally revealed* law of the Jews contained in the Old Testament] are a law to themselves, who show the work of the law [the *externally revealed* law of the Jews contained in the Old Testament] written in their hearts, their conscience also bearing witness. . . ."

---

4. Handley C.G. Moule, *The Epistle to the Romans*, (London, England: Pickering & Inglis Ltd., nd), 65.

Commenting on this passage, Robert Haldane says, "This evidently shows that they have a law, the work of which is written in their hearts, by which they discern the difference between right and wrong—what is just, and what is unjust."[5] John Murray agrees when he says, ". . . although the Gentiles are 'without the law' and 'have not the law' in the sense of specially revealed law, nevertheless they are not entirely without law; the law is made known to them and is brought to bear upon them in another way."[6] Gentiles without special revelation were not, and are not, without law absolutely.

3. What law do Gentiles without special revelation possess?

It should be obvious now that what the Gentiles possess is the Ten Commandments, though not necessarily in the identical *form* as they appear in the Decalogue. This is why some have sought to show that the essence of the Decalogue is found scattered throughout the book of Genesis. This would prove that

5. Robert Haldane, *An Exposition of the Epistle to the Romans*, (Mac Dill AFB, Florida: Mac Donald Publishing Company, nd), 90.

6. John Murray, *The Epistle to the Romans*, (Grand Rapids, MI: Wm. B. Eerdmans Publishing Co., re. 1984), 72. On page 74, commenting on verse 14, Murray says, "The omission of the definite article before . . . [law] on three occasions in verse 14 is an interesting example of the omission when the subject is specific and definite. On the first two occasions the law in mind is the specially revealed law as exemplified in Scripture. That it is definite is shown by the expression . . . [the things of the law]. For this reason we should most reasonably take . . . [law] in the concluding clause as definite—the Gentiles are not simply *a* law to themselves but *the* law spoken of in the other clauses of the verse. This is confirmed by verse 15 where we have the expression . . . [the work of the law]. The point is that it is not an entirely different law with which the Gentiles are confronted; the things of the law they do are not things of an entirely different law—it is essentially the same law. The difference resides in the different *method* [emphasis added] of being confronted with it and, by implication, in the less detailed and perspicuous knowledge of its content." See also Frederic Louis Godet, *Commentary on Romans*, (Grand Rapids, MI: Kregel Publications, re. 1979), 124, where he says that the Gentiles "have it [the law the Jews possess] in another way" and ". . . he [Paul] wishes to establish the identity of the Gentile's moral instinct with the contents of the *Mosaic* [emphasis Godet's] law strictly so called."

the individual commands of the entire Decalogue were the expected ethical norms for man before the promulgation of the summarization of the Moral Law in the form of the Decalogue via Moses.[7] In other words, what the Jews get via special revelation the Gentiles get via general revelation. They get the same law but through different means of revelation and in a different form.[8] The great Reformed theologian Francis Turretin agrees.

> If it is asked how this natural law agrees with or differs from the moral law [the moral law in the context of Turretin's statement refers to the Decalogue], the answer is easy. It agrees as to substance and with regard to principles, but differs as to

---

7. See for instance, F. W. Farrar, *The Voice from Sinai*, (New York, NY: Thomas Whittaker, 1892), 4. Farrar says, ". . . the moral law of Sinai, written on the tablets of stone, was, as Bishop Andrewes points out, a promulgation of the law always written on the fleshen tables of the heart. Thus (he says) we have all the Ten Commandments in Genesis. . . ." See also Walter C. Kaiser, Jr., *Toward Old Testament Ethics*, (Grand Rapids, MI: Zondervan Publishing House, 1991), 81–82, where he says, "In spite of its marvelous succinctness, economy of words, and comprehensive vision, it must not be thought that the Decalogue was inaugurated and promulgated at Sinai for the first time. All Ten Commandments had been part of the law of God previously written on hearts instead of stone, for all ten appear, in one way or another, in Genesis. They are: The first, Genesis 35:2 . . . The second, Genesis 31:39 . . . The third, Genesis 24:3 . . . The fourth, Genesis 2:3 . . . The fifth, Genesis 27:41 . . . The sixth, Genesis 4:9 . . . The seventh, Genesis 39:9 . . . The eighth, Genesis 44:4–7 . . . The ninth, Genesis 39:17 . . . The tenth, Genesis 12:18; 20:3." See Ernest C. Reisinger, *The Law and the Gospel*, (Phillipsburg, NJ: P&R Publishing, 1997), 18–22, for an attempt to show "that the violation of each of the Ten Commandments was either severely punished or openly rebuked before Sinai." *Ibid*, 18.

8. Douglas Moo adds, "'The things of the law' is a general way of stating certain of those requirements of the Mosaic law that God has made universally available to human beings in their very constitution. Paul's point is that Gentiles outside of Christ regularly obey their parents, refrain from murder and robbery, and so on." Douglas Moo, *The Epistle to the Romans*, (Grand Rapids, MI: Wm. B. Eerdmans Publishing Company, 1996), 150. In footnote 38, on the same page, Moo adds, "Paul is therefore clearly thinking here mainly of what has traditionally been called the 'moral' dimensions of the law. . . ." However, Moo does not identify what the Gentiles have as the natural form of the Decalogue.

accidents and with regard to conclusions. The same duties (both toward God and toward our neighbor) prescribed by the moral law are also contained in the natural law. The difference is with regard to the mode of delivery.[9]

Challenge to New Covenant Theology

New Covenant Theology's attempt to identify the Moral Law, or the law of God common to all men, complicates matters too much. It assumes a hermeneutic not based on exegesis. Instead, a careful exegesis of Romans 2:14–15 demonstrates that the Moral Law is summarily contained in the whole Decalogue and is at the same time common to all men through general revelation.

9. Francis Turretin, *Institutes of Elenctic Theology, Volume Two,* (Phillipsburg, NJ: P&R Publishing, 1994), 6.

6

New Covenant Theology and Hermeneutical Presuppositions

The Issue at Stake

A sixth area of challenge for New Covenant theologians concerns hermeneutical presuppositions. New Covenant Theology seems to hold to the maxim: Not repeated, not binding. Let me illustrate. New Covenant theologians say, "Since all of the Ten Commandments are not repeated in the New Testament, and only those repeated are still binding, therefore, not all ten are still binding." For instance, John Reisinger says, "Nine of the ten are repeated in the New Testament Scriptures and are *therefore* [emphasis added] just as binding on a Christian as they were on an Israelite."[1] This position is very common. Whatever is repeated in the New is for the Christian; whatever is not is fulfilled in Christ and not for the Christian. The historic Reformed hermeneutic assumes continuity between the testaments unless rescinded. New Covenant Theology assumes discontinuity unless repeated.

Challenge to New Covenant Theology

The first part of the New Covenant Theology claim is partially true and can be proven from the New Testament. To be sure, not all of the Ten Commandments are *explicitly repeated* in

---

1. Reisinger, *Tablets of Stone*, 99.

the New Testament. In fact, only the fifth through the ninth commandments are repeated this way.[2]

However, the second part of the New Covenant Theology claim is not true. It is simply not true that only those things from the Old Testament repeated in the New are still binding. Where is the exegetical basis for such a claim? There is none. Where does the New Testament tell us that the absence of Old Testament commands is the death knell of such commands? Would not this mean that only those verses of the book of Proverbs repeated in the New Testament are relevant for Christians? Nowhere in the New Testament does it tell us that Old Testament commands not repeated in the New Testament are not binding. How can Reisinger's "therefore," in the statement above, be justified from Scripture? It cannot.

Unfortunately, many Evangelical Christians adhere to this maxim today. Yet it is simply a hermeneutical presupposition, not based on the exegesis of the text of Scripture, but instead imposed on the Scripture. I have yet to see this maxim established from exegesis, and even when it is assumed, it is fraught with exegetical and practical difficulties.

---

2. In saying this, I am not denying that the first four commandments and the tenth are repeated in the New Testament. I believe they are though not in the *explicit form* in which they occur in the Decalogue.

7

New Covenant Theology and Canonics

The Issue at Stake

A seventh area of challenge for New Covenant Theology comes in the area of the canon of Scripture. *Canon* means rule or standard. The canon of Scripture is the sixty-six books of the Bible. All true Christians *formally* acknowledge that the sixty-six books contained in the Old and New Testaments (every chapter and every verse of every book) are the word of God. However, some Christians at least give the appearance of denying this *functionally*.

For instance, when it comes to ethics, New Covenant Theology says that ethics are based on the law Christ gives to us as the New Covenant lawgiver. New Covenant theologians seem to define "the law of Christ" to mean only our Lord's earthly teachings and the rest of the New Testament (which itself includes selective portions of the Old Testament). Their basic claim seems to be that only those portions of the Old Testament repeated in the New Testament become covenant law and are therefore binding for the Christian.

Challenge to New Covenant Theology

However, Christ taught us that the whole Old Testament, not just those portions repeated in the New Testament, had a place in His kingdom (Matt. 5:17–20). Paul, Christ's apostle to the Gentiles, also said that the whole Old Testament was "profitable for

. . . righteousness, that the man of God may be complete, thoroughly equipped for every good work" (2 Tim. 3:16–17). In context, he was saying that the whole Old Testament is profitable for the minister of the New Covenant.

The New Covenant Theology position, practically speaking, reduces the canon for ethics to the New Testament alone. As Zaspel says, "We would rather expect that for new covenant believers divine law would be codified in the new covenant."[1] Put another way, the New Covenant Theology position appears to leave us with a revelational canon—the Old and New Testaments—and an ethical canon—the New Testament. The canon of Scripture is *functionally* reduced in this approach. Ethical decisions can be biblically informed from certain sections of the Bible but not others. Moreover, this is so not because those other sections do not speak to the issue at hand, but because those other sections do not occur in the right section of Scripture, namely the New Testament. The first century Christians would have had a very small ethical canon to work with if they had held to this theory. There is little wonder that New Covenant Theology leaves itself open to the accusation of neo-Marcianism,[2] due to its reductionistic, myopic, and truncated approach to ethics.

---

1. Zaspel, "Divine Law," 155.
2. Marcion was a second century heretic who rejected the Old Testament and reduced the New Testament canon to an abbreviated Gospel of Luke and ten Pauline epistles.

8

New Covenant Theology and Historical Theology

The Issue at Stake

A final area of challenge for New Covenant Theology concerns its understanding of historical theology. We will examine three areas of concern: first, New Covenant Theology's understanding of *The Baptist Confession of Faith of 1689* on the law of God; second, New Covenant Theology's understanding of John Calvin on the Decalogue and the Sabbath; and third, New Covenant Theology's understanding of John Bunyan on the Sabbath.

The Baptist Confession of Faith on the Law of God

The Baptist Confession of Faith of 1689 is a daughter confession of *The Westminster Confession of Faith* and is in substantial agreement with it on the subject of the law of God. New Covenant theologians often chide these historic Reformed confessions concerning their view of the relationship between Old Covenant and New Covenant law. Because both confessions hold to the transcovenantal utility of the Decalogue, they are claimed to be flat in their approach to the issues related to continuity and discontinuity.

However, continuity in law and discontinuity in application due to the redemptive-historical effects brought on by Christ's death and the inauguration of the New Covenant are both acknowledged in these confessions, though not in those words. Both *The Westminster Confession of Faith* and *The Baptist Confession of*

Faith of 1689 acknowledge that Christ demands more of His people in light of His coming. Both confessions read as follows in 19:5.

> The moral law doth for ever bind all, as well justified persons as others, to the obedience thereof, and that not only in regard of the matter contained in it, but also in respect of the authority of God the Creator, who gave it; neither doth Christ in the Gospel any way dissolve, but much *strengthen this obligation.*

The Baptist Confession of Faith of 1689 in 19:3 also acknowledges that Christ is "the true Messiah and *only law-giver* [emphasis added]. . . ." Thus, neither confession takes a flat view of the relationship between Old Covenant and New Covenant law. Indeed, the very acknowledgment that Christ strengthens our obligation to the Moral Law (Decalogue in context) under the New Covenant in 19:5 and the change of the Sabbath from the seventh to the first day in 22:7[1] demonstrates that both confessions recognize redemptive-historical changes in the application of the Decalogue since the coming of Christ.

In addition, statements in 19:3 and 19:4 testify to an acknowledgment of a shift in the application of law during the inter-adventual period by stating that the "ceremonial laws" of the Old Covenant have been "abrogated"[2] and that the general equity of the "judicial laws" are still of use. The seventeenth-century men who drafted these confessions saw redemptive-historical effects produced by Christ's death and the inauguration of the New Covenant and included this perspective in their confessional statements.

---

1. This occurs in 21:7 in the Westminster Confession.

2. It is of interest to note that the BCF 1689 in 19:3 says that the "ceremonial laws, . . . are by Jesus Christ the true Messiah and *only law-giver* [emphasis added], . . . abrogated and taken away" and in 28:1 that "Baptism and the Lord's supper are ordinances of positive and sovereign institution, appointed by the Lord Jesus, *the only lawgiver* [emphasis added]. . . ."

Challenge to New Covenant Theology

We can conclude, then, that the New Covenant Theology claim that these confessions are flat in their approach to the issues related to Old and New Covenant law does not do justice to the confessions' words, but gives the appearance of reading one's theology back into theirs. New Covenant Theology's contention that these confessions are Old Covenant in their approach to biblical law is unfounded and oversimplifies their statements.

JOHN CALVIN ON THE DECALOGUE AND THE SABBATH

Another area of challenge for New Covenant Theology in the area of historical theology concerns John Calvin on the Decalogue and the Sabbath.[3] New Covenant theologians frequently appeal to John Calvin to support their views. They represent him to have been strictly anti-Sabbatarian in his view of the perpetuity of the fourth commandment. More specifically, they say that Calvin believed the fourth commandment was a temporary law exclusively regulating the Jews under the Old Covenant. They thus claim to be heirs of Calvin and the continental Reformers in holding that the New Covenant's Lord's Day is not Sabbath directed. For example, Fred Zaspel claims, ". . . the sabbatarian is not properly a 'Reformed' position, for the continental Reformers themselves did not so observe the day."[4]

However, Calvin's views of the Natural Law, the transcovenantal utility of the Decalogue, and the function of the fourth commandment under the New Covenant seriously undermine this position. To be sure, we cannot say that Calvin was a Sabbatarian without qualification, but certainly, his view is more complex than Zaspel's statement reflects. As shown below, it is overly simplistic for either anti-Sabbatarians or Sabbatarians to claim Calvin as their own. As with many difficult theological issues, Calvin steers a middle road between what

---

3. Most of this section was originally written toward the completion of the Post-Graduate Degree Program at Whitefield Theological Seminary as a prerequisite for doctoral studies.

4. Zaspel, "Divine Law," 168, n. 40.

he considered as excess on both sides. We must respect Calvin for his attempts to synthesize all the relevant biblical data concerning these issues, though we may not agree with all of his conclusions.

CALVIN ON THE DECALOGUE AND THE NATURAL LAW

Calvin very clearly and in many places identified the Decalogue as a special form of the natural law. For instance, Calvin said, "Now that inward law, which we have above described as written, even engraved, upon the hearts of all, in a sense asserts the very same things that are to be learned from the two Tables."[5] Calvin "saw the revealed law as given in the Ten Commandments as a specially accommodated restatement of the law of nature for the Jews."[6] He clearly held that by nature Gentiles without special revelation possessed the general knowledge of the Decalogue, though obscured by sin.[7] I. John Hesselink says, "There is no denying that for Calvin the content of the moral law is essentially the same as that inscribed on the hearts of

---

5. Calvin, *Institutes of the Christian Religion,* (Philadelphia, PA: The Westminster Press, 1960), 367–368. This was Luther's position as well according to Paul Althaus in *The Ethics of Martin Luther.* He says, "The law written in man's heart contains within itself all the commandments of the First and Second Tables . . . Luther highly praises the law of Moses as the most striking form of the natural law. He calls it 'a summary of divine teaching' that comprehends the entire content of the law. All good works must have their source here; nothing that is God–pleasing lies outside the sphere of the Ten Commandments. 'Therefore we should prize and value them above all other teachings as the greatest treasure God has given us.'" Althaus, *The Ethics of Martin Luther,* 28, 30.

6. I. John Hesselink, *Calvin's Concept of the Law,* (Allison Park, PA: Pickwick Publications, 1992), 51.

7. In Calvin, *Institutes,* 368, while introducing the Ten Commandments, he says, ". . . the Lord has provided us with a written law to give us a clearer witness of what was too obscure in the natural law, . . ." He uses the phrases "rule of perfect righteousness"(371), "the law of the Lord"(372), "individual articles [of the law of the Lord]"(372), "the commandments"(375), "two Tables"(376), all referring to the Decalogue. The natural law and written law [Ten Commandments] are identical in substance though different in form.

humans 'by nature.'"[8] Francois Wendel says, "One can even say that, for Calvin, the Decalogue is only a special application of the natural law which God came to attest and confirm."[9]

Calvin's view of the transcovenantal utility of the Decalogue is no secret. In the 1559 edition of the Institutes of the Christian Religion, Calvin clearly upheld the perpetuity of both Tables of the law for New Covenant believers.[10] For instance, he says:

> The whole law is contained under two heads. Yet our God, to remove all possibility of excuse, willed to set forth more fully and clearly by the Ten Commandments everything connected with the honor, fear, and love of him, and everything pertaining to the love toward men, which he for his own sake enjoins upon us.[11]

Accordingly, Calvin clearly held that the Decalogue, all Ten Commandments, functioned as the basic, fundamental law of the Bible and as a universal ethical canon for all men based on creation.

CALVIN AND THE SABBATH

These perspectives must be understood in order to understand Calvin's view of the Sabbath. Calvin viewed the fourth commandment as part of the law that is transcovenantal and common to all men. Therefore, any understanding of Calvin that quickly dismisses him from the ranks of those who hold to the perpetuity of the fourth commandment will be found wanting. If New Covenant theologians dismiss Calvin from such ranks, then they are misinformed and need to go *ad fontes* (to the sources).

New Covenant Theology seems to claim that Calvin believed the fourth commandment was fulfilled in Christ and no longer

---

8. Hesselink, *Calvin's ...Law*, 10.

9. Francois Wendel, *Calvin, Origins and Developments of His Religious Thought*, (Grand Rapids, MI: Baker Book House, re. 1997), 206.

10. Calvin, *Institutes*, 361.

11. *Ibid*, 376–377.

functions to regulate the Lord's Day under the New Covenant. This understanding leads some New Covenant theologians to say that the Lord's Day is not Sabbath-directed. However, once again, Calvin's position is more involved than that.

Calvin's understanding of the Sabbath does not start with redemption in Exodus 20, but with creation in Genesis 2. Commenting on Genesis 2:3, Calvin says:

> . . . we must know, that this is to be the common employment not of one age or people only, but of the whole human race. Afterwards in the Law, a new precept concerning the Sabbath was given, which should be peculiar to the Jews, and but for a season . . . Therefore when we hear that the Sabbath was abrogated by the coming of Christ, we must distinguish between what belongs to the perpetual governments of human life, and what properly belongs to ancient figures, the use of which was abolished when the truth was fulfilled. . . . So far as the Sabbath was a figure of this rest, I say, it was but for a season; but in as much as it was commanded to men from the beginning that they might employ themselves in the worship of God, it is right that it should continue to the end of the world.[12]

There is evidence elsewhere in his writings that Calvin believed the Sabbath predated the promulgation of the Decalogue. For instance, commenting on Exodus 20:11, he says:

> From this passage it may be probably conjectured that the hallowing of the Sabbath was prior to the Law; and undoubtedly what Moses has before narrated [Exodus 16], that they were forbidden to gather the manna on the seventh day, seems to have had its origin from a well-known and received custom; whilst it is not credible that the observance of the Sabbath was omitted, when God revealed the rite of sacrifice to the holy (Fathers.) But what in the depravity of human na-

---

12. Calvin, *Calvin's Commentaries, Volume I, Genesis*, (Grand Rapids, MI: Baker Book House, re. 1984), 106–107.

ture was altogether extinct among heathen nations, and almost obsolete with the race of Abraham, God, renewed in His Law: that the Sabbath should be honoured by holy and inviolable observance. . . .[13]

In his *Commentary on the Last Four Books of Moses* published in 1563[14] Calvin asserts:

I do not, however, doubt but that God created the world in six days and rested on the seventh, that He might give a manifestation of the perfect excellency of His works, and thus, proposing Himself as the model for our imitation, He signifies that He calls His own people to the true goal of felicity.[15]

Concerning the fourth commandment and ceremonial abrogation, Calvin says, ". . . there is no doubt that by the Lord Christ's coming the *ceremonial part*[16] of this commandment was abolished. . . . Christians ought therefore to shun completely the superstitious observance of days."[17] However, to take this as stripping the fourth commandment of moral and perpetual use, as many New Covenant theologians have done, is to misunderstand Calvin. Listen to him.

When I said that the ordinance of rest was a type of a spiritual and far higher mystery, and hence that this Commandment

---

13. Calvin, *Calvin's Commentaries, Volume II, Harmony of Exodus, Leviticus, Numbers, Deuteronomy,* (Grand Rapids, MI: Baker Book House, 1984), 439–440.

14. This date is crucial. The definitive edition of the *Institutes* was published in 1559 and the *Harmony* was published the year before Calvin's death. It is necessary to consider this when seeking to establish a comprehensive view of Calvin's mature thoughts on the Sabbath.

15. Calvin, *Calvin's Commentaries Volume II,* 436.

16. For Calvin, the ceremonial part of the fourth commandment referred primarily to its forward look prefiguring eternal rest fulfilled in Christ and secondarily to the distinguishing of one day above another based on the commandment itself.

17. Calvin, *Institutes,* 397.

must be counted ceremonial, I must not be supposed to mean
that it had no other different objects also.[18]

The two latter reasons for the Sabbath [a stated day for public worship and a day of rest for servants] ought not to be
relegated to the ancient shadows, but are *equally applicable
to every age* [emphasis added]. Although the Sabbath has
been abrogated, there is still occasion for us: (1) to assemble
on stated days for the hearing of the Word, the breaking of
the mystical bread, and for public prayers. . . . ; (2) to give
surcease from labor to servants and workmen. There is no
doubt that in enjoining the Sabbath the Lord was concerned
with both. . . . Who can deny that these things apply as
much to us as to the Jews? Meetings of the church are en-
joined upon us by God's Word; and from our everyday ex-
perience we well know how we need them. But how can
such meetings be held unless they have been established
and have their stated days? According to the apostle's statement, "all things should be done decently and in order"
among us. It is so impossible to maintain decency and order—otherwise than by this arrangement and regulation—
that immediate confusion and ruin threaten the church if it
be dissolved. But if we are subject to the same necessity as
that to alleviate which the Lord established the Sabbath for
the Jews, let no one allege that this has nothing to do with
us. For our most provident and merciful father willed to see
our needs not less than those of the Jews.[19]

Some observations may be helpful at this point. First, Calvin
believed the fourth commandment's provisions of a day of public worship and physical rest from normal labors apply to every
age. Second, Calvin believed that certain elements of the fourth
commandment may be abrogated without necessarily abrogat-
ing all of the elements of the fourth commandment.[20] And third,
Calvin believed that the fourth commandment has something

18. Calvin, *Calvin's Commentaries Volume II*, 437.
19. Calvin, *Institutes*, 397–398.
20. This is why you will hear Calvin say *the Sabbath has been abrogated*
on the one hand, and *let no one allege that this* [the Sabbath as established
for the Jews and contained in the fourth commandment] *has nothing to do*

to do with Christians.[21] This vital text from the *Institutes* referenced above should silence those who make hasty generaliza-
tions about Calvin being anti-Sabbatarian.

Is Calvin anti-sabbatarian?

So is Calvin anti-Sabbatarian? In one sense, yes, and in another, no. Calvin is difficult to sort out at times concerning ceremonial abrogation and moral perpetuity. For instance, in one
place in the *Institutes,* he says:

> Thus vanish the trifles of the false prophets, who in former
> centuries infected the people with a Jewish opinion. They
> asserted that nothing but the ceremonial part of this com-
> mandment has been abrogated (in their phraseology the "ap-
> pointing" of the seventh day), but the moral part remains—
> namely, the fixing of one day in seven.[22]

Calvin uses the same paradigm of ceremonial abrogation and
moral perpetuity but applies it differently. Moral perpetuity
and the fourth commandment to Calvin seem to be limited to
the protection of the public worship of God. His last statement
in his exposition of the Decalogue in his *Institutes* is telling.
After rebuking *crass and carnal Sabbatarian superstition* (i.e.,
medieval ecclesiastically sanctioned legalistic encumbrances,
in the words of Gaffin), he says:

---

with us. Concerning the phenomenon of abrogation as it relates to the Sabbath in the Genevan Catechism of 1545 written by Calvin, Richard B. Gaffin
says, ". . . the statements in which Calvin speaks of the abrogation of the
Sabbath or the temporary character of the fourth commandment are subject
to immediate qualification. Such qualification is most explicit here. It is
only the Sabbath narrowly considered in terms of its ceremonial character
and the fourth commandment contemplated as prescribing this ceremony
which are said to be abolished. Furthermore, it is immediately added that
there is more involved in the fourth commandment than a ceremonial ordinance." Richard B. Gaffin, *Calvin and the Sabbath,* (Scarsdale, NY:
Westminster Discount Book Service, 1981), 44–45.   ˙

21. I take *us* in the context of Calvin's statement above to refer to Christians under the New Covenant.

22. Calvin, *Institutes,* 400.

But we ought especially to hold to this general doctrine: that, in order to prevent religion from either perishing or declining among us, we should diligently frequent the sacred meetings, and make use of those external aids which can promote the worship of God[23]

Richard B. Gaffin's comments are appropriate here.

The very last sentence of the exposition [of the fourth commandment in the *Institutes*] is worth quoting because it gives in kernel form, after all discussion has been completed, just what Calvin thinks is the most important single practical element in the teaching of the fourth commandment, what above all else this commandment requires of the believer today. "But we ought especially to hold to this general doctrine: that, in order to prevent religion from either perishing or declining among us, we should diligently frequent the sacred meetings, and make use of those external aids which can promote the worship of God." That which is indicated by the tenor of his whole discussion is now expressly affirmed. For Calvin the preeminent practical concern of the fourth commandment is the maintenance of public worship.[24]

CALVIN ON THE SABBATH AND THE LORD'S DAY.

The relationship between the Old Covenant Sabbath and the New Covenant Lord's Day is a concept articulated more clearly in the seventeenth century than in the sixteenth. However, traces of Calvin's perspective are detectable. In the *Institutes,* probably speaking against antinomianism, he says:

. . . we transcend Judaism in observing these days [in context "these days" refers to Lord's Days] because we are far different from the Jews in this respect. For we are not celebrating it as a ceremony with the most rigid scrupulousness, supposing a spiritual mystery to be figured thereby.

---

23. Calvin, *Institutes*, 401.

24. Gaffin, *Calvin . . . Sabbath*, 29. The sentence by Calvin can be found in Calvin, *Institutes*, 401.

Rather, we are using it as a remedy needed to keep order in the church.[25]

In his commentary on Luke 4:16, he says:

Hence also it is evident, what was the true and lawful method of keeping the Sabbath. When God commanded his people to abstain from working on that day, it was not that they might give themselves up to indolent repose, but, on the contrary, that they might exercise themselves in meditating on his works. Now, the minds of men are naturally blind to the consideration of his works, and must therefore be guided by the rule of Scripture. Though Paul includes the Sabbath in an enumeration of the shadows of the law, (Col. ii. 16,) yet, in this respect, our manner of observing it is the same with that of the Jews: the people must assemble to hear the word, to public prayers, and to the other exercises of religion. It was for this purpose that the Jewish Sabbath was succeeded by the Lord's Day.[26]

It would appear that Calvin's view of the relationship between the seventh day Sabbath and the first-day Lord's Day is not one of strict replacement. The authority for meeting on the seventh day is based on the explicit special revelation of the Old Testament, but the authority for meeting on the first day is not so clearly ascertainable in Calvin's thought.

Challenge to New Covenant Theology

It now becomes clear that Calvin was neither New Covenant in his view of the Sabbath/ Lord's Day question, nor was he perfectly in line with the confessional theology of the seventeenth century. Calvin's view of the Sabbath was very complex and cannot be claimed by either New Covenant Theology or those adhering to the Puritan view of the Sabbath. He believed that the

25. Calvin, *Institutes*, 399.
26. Calvin, *Calvin's Commentaries, Volume XVI, Harmony of Matthew, Mark, Luke,* (Grand Rapids, MI: Baker Book House, 1984), 227.

Sabbath was rooted in creation and was for all men; that the fourth commandment was part of the natural law written on the hearts of all men; that the Sabbath took on unique and temporary features under the Mosaic economy; that the ceremonial aspects of the Old Covenant Sabbath were and are fulfilled in Christ; that the fourth commandment functions under the New Covenant to protect the public worship of God; that the best day to meet for public worship under the New Covenant is the first day of the week, though not based on Scriptural command.

If New Covenant theologians want to claim to be heirs of Calvin when it comes to their view of the Sabbath, then they must be willing to acknowledge that the Sabbath was given in the Garden and is for all ages and all men, and that the fourth commandment still regulates the meetings of the church for corporate worship. But this would be tantamount to denying basic tenets of New Covenant Theology. We can safely conclude that New Covenant Theology does not bear the mantle of John Calvin when it comes to the issue of the Sabbath.

JOHN BUNYAN ON THE SABBATH

A final area of challenge in the field of historical theology for New Covenant Theology concerns John Bunyan on the Sabbath. New Covenant theologians lean upon their understanding of John Bunyan's view of the Sabbath and use him as another historical precedent for their position, at least in part.[27] It is claimed that Bunyan broke rank with his contemporary Puritan brethren on the issue of the Sabbath. Bunyan's denial of the perpetuity of the seventh day Sabbath from creation to

---

27. John Reisinger has an article entitled *John Bunyan on the Sabbath*. The article is available from Sound of Grace, PO Box 185, Webster, NY 14580. In it he makes many of the observations I make on Bunyan's view of the Sabbath. He shows that Bunyan did not believe the Sabbath was a Creation Ordinance and that Bunyan believed the Lord's Day to be the Christian Sabbath. Reisinger's article concentrates on Bunyan's arguments against the Sabbath as a Creation Ordinance. However, Bunyan's own treatise is comprised of ten pages seeking to prove that the *seventh day* (emphasis mine, and crucial) Sabbath was not given until Sinai, and therefore not Moral Law, and fourteen pages seeking to prove that the Lord's Day is the Christian Sabbath.

the resurrection of Christ was used to drive a wedge between him and his Puritan brethren. Bunyan is then claimed as a forerunner to New Covenant Theology's perspective on the Sabbath question. However, as with Calvin, things just aren't that simple. The full title of Bunyan's treatment of the Sabbath question is: *Questions about the Nature and Perpetuity of the Seventh day Sabbath and proof that the First Day of the Week is the True Christian Sabbath.* Bunyan's purpose in writing is clear in his title. When Bunyan says he is going to deal with the seventh day Sabbath, his seventeenth-century audience would have immediately known what he meant. He was not combating the Puritan view of the Sabbath as articulated in *The Westminster Confession of Faith* or *The Baptist Confession of Faith of 1689*, but writing against a movement that sought to impose the *seventh day* Sabbath as Moral Law upon Christians. This is stated in the Editor's Advertisement of the 1854 edition of Bunyan's works:

> In 1628, Mr. Brabourne, a clergyman of note, kept the Jewish Sabbath, and in a short time several churches, in England, assembled on that day, and were called "seventh day, or Sabbath keepers"—many of them were Baptists. This led to the controversy in which Bunyan took his part, in this very conclusive and admirable treatise.[28]

Bunyan was writing against a movement that sought to identify the Christian day of worship as the *seventh day* Sabbath. Later in the century, Baptists who held to this were called Seventh Day Baptists. His purpose in writing, then, was two-fold: first, to refute the view that the seventh day of the week is the Christian Sabbath; and second, to offer proof that the first day of the week is the Christian Sabbath. He wanted to offer "proof that the first day of the week is the Christian sabbath"[29], while acknowledging that "God's church has already been so well fur-

---

28. John Bunyan, *The Works of John Bunyan, Volume Two*, (Carlisle, PA: The Banner of Truth Trust, 1991), 360.
29. *Ibid*, 361.

nished with sound grounds and reasons by so many wise and godly men."[30]

Bunyan clearly denied that the *seventh day* of the week is Moral Law. He says, "The seventh day sabbath was not moral."[31] He also did not believe that God gave the *seventh day* as a Sabbath rest before the promulgation of the Decalogue. He says:

> It follows therefore, that if the law of nature doth not of itself reveal to us, as men, that *the seventh day* [emphasis added] is the holy sabbath of God. That that day, as to the sanction of it, is not moral, but rather arbitrary, to wit, imposed by the will of God upon his people, until the time he thought fit to change it for another day.[32]

He states very clearly that he did not believe the *seventh day* Sabbath to be Moral Law or the law of nature. However, this does not mean that the Sabbath concept itself is not Moral Law. Listen to Bunyan again.

> I have here, by handling four questions, proved, that the seventh day sabbath was not moral. For that must of necessity be done, before it can be made appear that the first day of the week is that which is the sabbath day for Christians. But withal it follows, that if the seventh day sabbath was not moral, the first day is not so. What is it then? *Why, a sabbath for holy worship is moral* [emphasis added]; but *this* or *that* day appointed for such service, is sanctified by precept or by approved example. The timing then of a sabbath for us lies in God. . . .[33]

Bunyan obviously believed that a Sabbath for worship was part of the Moral Law, but that the day for such a Sabbath was not.

---

30. John Bunyan, *The Works of John Bunyan, Volume Two*, (Carlisle, PA: The Banner of Truth Trust, 1991), 361.

31. Bunyan, *Works, Volume Two*, 361.

32. *Ibid.*

33. *Ibid*, 361. This was written in 1685 and reflects Bunyan's mature thought on the Sabbath as Moral Law.

That demanded positive law. Bunyan was combating the view that *the seventh day of the week* is moral, and therefore perpetually binding on all men. He acknowledged that a Sabbath for worship is moral, but not *the seventh day of the week*. Elsewhere he says, "*Time* to worship God in, is required by the law of nature; but that the law of nature doth, as such, fix it on the seventh day from the creation of the world, that I utterly deny. . . ."[34]

It is true that Bunyan did not hold to the majority Puritan position on the Sabbath at creation. He did not see a positive command in the account of creation nor an approved example that sanctified the seventh day. He clearly did not hold to the position of *The Westminster Confession* or *The Baptist Confession of Faith of 1689* in his treatise on the Sabbath. However, Bunyan seems to contradict himself elsewhere.

For instance, in his *The Doctrine of the Law and Grace Unfolded*, he makes *many* statements difficult to reconcile with his contention that the seventh day Sabbath was not revealed until the tablets of stone were given to Moses. He says:

> though this law [the law of the covenant of works] was delivered to Moses from the hands of angels in two tables of stone, on Mount Sinai, yet this was not the first appearing of this law to man; but even this in substance, though possibly not so openly, was given to the first man, Adam, in the garden of Eden. . . .[35]

> God commanded Adam in paradise to abstain from all evil against the first covenant, and not from some sins only; but if God had not commanded Adam to abstain from the sins spoken against in the ten commandments, he had not commanded to abstain from all, but from some; therefore it must needs be that he then commanded to abstain from all sins

---

34. Bunyan, *Works, Volume Two*, 371.
35. John Bunyan, *The Works of John Bunyan, Volume One*, (Carlisle, PA: The Banner of Truth Trust, 1991), 498.

forbidden in the law given on Mount Sinai. Now that God commanded to abstain from all evil or sin against any of the ten commandments, when he gave Adam the command in the garden, it is evident in that he did punish the sins that were committed against those commands that were then delivered on Mount Sinai, which will appear as followeth . . .[36]

Bunyan then attempts to show that God punished the sins that were committed against all Ten Commandments prior to the promulgation of the Decalogue on Sinai. Of special interest is the fact that he says, "we find the Lord rebuking his people for the breach of the fourth commandment. Ex. xvi. 27–29."[37] This appears to contradict what Bunyan says in his treatise on the Sabbath. How are we to reconcile these statements?

In his treatises on the Sabbath, Bunyan argued that since we do not see sins against the *seventh day* Sabbath punished prior to the giving of the law on tablets of stone, then the *seventh day* Sabbath is not Moral Law. He does not, however, deny that the Sabbath is Moral Law. In fact, he says, "a sabbath for holy worship is moral."[38] In his treatise on law and grace he clearly affirms that the Decalogue, in substance, predates the tablets of stone. Listen to Bunyan.

. . . in that death did reign from Adam to Moses, or from the time of his transgression against the first giving of the law, till the time the law was given on Mount Sinai, it is evident that the substance of the ten commandments was given to Adam and his posterity. . . .[39]

. . . they are no other sins than those against that law given on Sinai, for the which those sins before mentioned were punished; therefore the law given before by the Lord to Adam and his posterity is the same with that afterwards given on Mount Sinai.[40]

---

36. John Bunyan, *The Works of John Bunyan, Volume One*, (Carlisle, PA: The Banner of Truth Trust, 1991), 498.
37. Bunyan, *Works, Volume One*, 499.
38. Bunyan, *Works, Volume Two*, 361.
39. Bunyan, *Works, Volume One*, 499.
40. *Ibid.*

Now the law given on Sinai was for the more clear discovery
of those sins that were before committed against it; for though
the very substance of the ten commandments were given in
the garden before they were received from Sinai . . .[41]
Therefore that which was delivered in two tables of stone on
Mount Sinai, is the very same that was given before to Adam
in paradise.[42]

Because Bunyan believed the Decalogue predated the tablets of stone, he could say, "we find the Lord rebuking his people
for the breach of the fourth commandment. Ex. xvi. 27–29."[43]
Notice he did not say, "we find the Lord rebuking his people for
the breach of the seventh day Sabbath." The seventh day Sabbath, in Bunyan's thought, was not given until Mount Sinai; but
a Sabbath for holy worship was demanded by the law of nature
and the terms of the covenant between God and Adam as the
representative of all mankind. On the one hand, a Sabbath for
worship is Moral Law and binding on all men. On the other
hand, the seventh day Sabbath is positive law and awaited the
giving of the law on tablets of stone. Either we understand
Bunyan this way or we conclude that he contradicted himself or
changed his views.

In any event, Bunyan clearly held that the Lord's Day is the
Christian Sabbath. He says this several times in the treaties on
the Sabbath. "[T]he first day of the week is that which is the
sabbath day for Christians."[44] Commenting on Revelation 1:10,
he says, "[T]he first day of the week is to be accounted the
Christian sabbath, or holy day for divine worship in the
churches of the saints."[45] He uses the following texts to support his view: Psalm 118:24; Isaiah 56:1–2; Matthew 12:8; John
20; Acts 20:7; 1 Corinthians 16:1–2; Hebrews 4:10; and Rev-

41. Bunyan, *Works, Volume One*, 500.
42. *Ibid.*
43. *Ibid*, 499.
44. Bunyan, *Works, Volume Two*, 361.
45. *Ibid*, 374.

elation 1:10. The only difference between Bunyan and the Puritan confessions seems to be his denial of the *seventh day* Sabbath as a positive law from creation to the resurrection.[46] However, he did acknowledge that "a sabbath for holy worship is moral."[47]

Challenge to New Covenant Theology

We are now prepared to ask the following question to New Covenant theologians: Does John Bunyan's view of the Sabbath accurately reflect New Covenant Theology? Does New Covenant Theology teach that "a Sabbath for worship is moral?"[48] Does New Covenant Theology teach that "the first day of the week is to be accounted the Christian Sabbath?" Does New Covenant Theology teach that "Christ rested from his own works as God did from his, therefore he also gave the day in which he rested from his works, a Sabbath to the churches, as did the Father?"[49] Does New Covenant Theology teach that the Lord's Day, "the *whole* day [emphasis Bunyan's],"[50] is to be set apart for solemn worship? Does New Covenant Theology teach that "there was given even by the apostles themselves, a holy respect to the first

---

46. *The Baptist Confession of Faith of 1689*, 22:7 reads: "As it is the law of nature, that in general a proportion of time, by God's appointment, be set apart for the worship of God, so by his Word, in a positive, moral, and perpetual commandment, binding all men in all ages, he hath particularly appointed one day in seven for a sabbath to be kept holy unto him, which from the beginning of the world to the resurrection of Christ was the last day of the week, and from the resurrection of Christ was changed into the first day of the week, which is called the Lord's Day: and is to be continued to the end of the world as the Christian Sabbath, the observation of the last day of the week being abolished."

47. Bunyan, *Works, Volume Two*, 361.

48. John Reisinger claims, "His [Bunyan's] basic view of the *nature* [emphasis mine] and *origin* [emphasis mine] of the Sabbath commandment is exactly what I believe." Reisinger, *John Bunyan on the Sabbath*, 3. In light of Bunyan's comment above concerning a Sabbath for worship being moral, one wonders if Reisinger overstated his case.

49. Bunyan, *Works, Volume Two*, 371–372.

50. *Ibid*, 376. Bunyan also says that we are "to fill up" the Lord's Day with solemn worship.

day of the week above all the days of the week?"[51] Does New Covenant Theology teach that "things done on the Lord's day, are better done, then on other days of the week, in his worship?"[52]

Some of these things are probably taught by New Covenant theologians, but certainly not all. Fairly stated, John Bunyan is not New Covenant in his view of the Sabbath. New Covenant Theology does not, as Bunyan did, teach that a Sabbath is Moral Law and part of the law of nature, that the first day of the week is the Christian Sabbath, otherwise called the Lord's Day, and that the Lord's Day, the first day of the week, is positive law sanctioned by Christ and his apostles "to the end of the world."[53]

In sum, although New Covenant Theology uses John Bunyan's arguments against the *seventh day* Sabbath to excuse the Sabbath from New Covenant law, this was not Bunyan's own position. Bunyan was not anti-Sabbatarian; he was anti-*seventh day*-Sabbatarian.

---

51. Bunyan, *Works, Volume Two*, 377.
52. *Ibid.*
53. *Ibid*, 378.

Conclusion

General Areas of Challenge to New Covenant Theology

This critique has presented eight broad areas of challenge to New Covenant Theology. I believe they are insuperable.

New Covenant Theology is to be commended for seeking to be sensitive to the newness of the New Covenant. However, at least in the field of ethics, it extends the concept of newness too far and ends up driving a wedge between Old and New Covenant law where God never put one.

New Covenant Theology also seeks to exalt Christ as our only lawgiver, which we applaud. But again, it extends this concept too far and ends up divorcing Christ from Moses in an artificial manner.

In the field of historical theology, New Covenant Theology gives the appearance of reading into history what it wants out of history.

Specific Areas of Challenge to New Covenant Theology

1) NEW COVENANT THEOLOGY AND EXEGETICAL THEOLOGY

The first level of challenge comes in the field of exegetical theology. New Covenant Theology's view of the law written on the heart under the New Covenant based on Jeremiah 31:33 does not adequately satisfy the language of the text. Also, New Covenant Theology's view of the Moral Law does not do justice to Romans 2:14–15 in the context of Paul's argument, nor to the broader context of Paul's theology concerning the place of the Decalogue in biblical ethics, nor to the teaching of the New Testament as a whole (see Rom. 3:19–20; 2 Cor. 3:3; Eph. 6:2–3; and 1 Tim. 1:8–11).

2) NEW COVENANT THEOLOGY AND BIBLICAL THEOLOGY

The second level of challenge to New Covenant Theology comes in the field of biblical theology. New Covenant Theology's position on the identity of the Old Covenant and the newness of the New Covenant ends up producing too much discontinuity between ethics under the Old and New Covenants. This makes New Covenant Theology sound like some older forms of Dispensational Theology when it comes to Christian ethics.

3) NEW COVENANT THEOLOGY AND HISTORICAL THEOLOGY

The third level of challenge to New Covenant Theology comes in the field of historical theology. New Covenant Theology does not do justice to either the seventeenth-century confessional theology of the Decalogue, John Calvin on the Decalogue and the Sabbath, or John Bunyan on the Sabbath.

4) NEW COVENANT THEOLOGY AND SYSTEMATIC THEOLOGY

The final level of challenge to New Covenant Theology comes in the field of systematic theology. With the problems associated with exegetical, biblical, and historical theology as stated above, it logically follows that New Covenant Theology is deficient in taking the fruits of these other disciplines within the theological curriculum and integrating them into a systematic whole that accurately conveys the meaning of the Bible. Systematic theology bases its conclusions on the fruit of these other disciplines, and when the fruit of these other disciplines is diseased, then the logical conclusions drawn from them will be diseased as well. This is the greatest concern we ought to have for New Covenant Theology; it ends up producing a diseased system of doctrine, which produces diseased Christian thinking and living.

Concluding Thoughts

It is the opinion of this writer that New Covenant Theology derives a set of exegetical axioms from various key texts and then imposes those axioms on the rest of the Bible. This produces a system which has the appearance of cogency based on the exegesis of Scripture. Cogency, of course, is what all Christians should strive for in their attempts to systematize Scripture. However, in the case of New Covenant Theology, the question to be asked is: Do the fundamental axioms of the system accurately reflect the teaching of Scripture? If the axioms are faulty, then the system is as well. In this critique, it is contended that the key exegetical axioms of New Covenant Theology are indeed faulty, do not stand up against the bar of Scripture, and thus, produce a faulty system. It is at this point where the crux of the matter lies: New Covenant Theology goes astray at the point of exegesis and thus produces a faulty theological system.

In saying these things, I am not saying that New Covenant Theology is totally fallacious. Many things taught by New Covenant Theology do accurately reflect the teaching of the Bible. However, there are some fundamental errors in the foundation, thus producing fundamental errors in the house. To the degree that the foundation is faulty, to that degree the system is faulty

The goal of this critique has been to fairly represent New Covenant Theology and present some challenges to it from a confessional Baptist perspective. To the best of the author's knowledge, he has sought to succeed at both and has offered what he trusts is a convincing case *In Defense of the Decalogue*. However, the real issue at stake here is the Bible itself, not the author's opinion. The questions to ask are: Does the Bible support the major tenets of New Covenant Theology critiqued here or not? Did this critique expose some insurmountable difficulties, which makes reconciling the claims of New Covenant Theology with the Bible impossible? Do the arguments presented here accurately reflect the teaching of the Bible? The reader is now encouraged to make the call himself with an open Bible and humble heart.

It is hoped that this critique will assist all interested Christians to wrestle with the difficult issues of continuity and discontinuity between the Testaments, to understand the function of the Ten Commandments in the history of redemption, and to arrive at a biblically consistent position. May the Lord so bless the endeavor.

Bibliography

Alford, Henry. *Alford's Greek Testament Volume III.* Grand Rapids, MI: Guardian Press, 1976.

Althaus, Paul. *The Ethics of Martin Luther.* Philadelphia, PA: Fortress Press, 1972.

Armstrong, John H., editor. *Reformation & Revival.* Volume 6, Number 3, Summer 1997. Carol Stream, IL: Reformation & Revival Ministries, Inc., 1997.

Arndt, William F., and F. Wilbur Gingrich, translators. *A Greek-English Lexicon of the New Testament and Other Early Christian Literature.* Chicago, IL: The University of Chicago Press, 1957.

Bernard, J.H. *Cambridge Greek Testament for Schools and Colleges, The Pastoral Epistles.* Cambridge, England: At the University Press, 1899.

Blass, F., and A. Debrunner. *A Greek Grammar of the New Testament and Other Early Christian Literature.* Chicago, IL: The University of Chicago Press, 1961.

Bromiley, Geoffrey W. *Theological Dictionary of the New Testament.* Grand Rapids, MI: Wm. B. Eerdmans Publishing Company, 1964, re. 1979.

Bunyan, John. *The Works of John Bunyan Volume One.* Carlisle, PA: The Banner of Truth Trust, 1991.

———. *The Works of John Bunyan Volume Two.* Carlisle, PA: The Banner of Truth Trust, 1991.

Bush, George. *Commentary on Exodus.* Grand Rapids, MI: Kregel Publications, re. 1993.

Calvin, John. *Calvin's Commentaries Volume I Genesis.* Grand Rapids, MI: Baker Book House, re. 1984.

————. *Calvin's Commentaries Volume II Harmony of Exodus, Leviticus, Numbers Deuteronomy.* Grand Rapids, MI: Baker Book House, 1984.

————. *Calvin's Commentaries, Volume XVI Harmony of Matthew, Mark, Luke.* Grand Rapids, MI: Baker Book House, re. 1984.

————. *Calvin's Commentaries Volume XX.* Grand Rapids, MI: Baker Book House, re. 1984.

————. *Institutes of the Christian Religion.* Philadelphia, PA: The Westminster Press, 1960.

Eadie, John. *Commentary on the Epistle to the Ephesians.* Minneapolis, MN: James and Klock Christian Publishing Co., re. 1977.

Fairbairn, Patrick. *The Pastoral Epistles.* Minneapolis, MN: Klock & Klock Christian Publishers, re. 1980.

Farrar, F.W. *The Voice from Sinai.* New York, NY: Thomas Whittaker, 1892.

Fisher, Edward. *The Marrow of Modern Divinity.* Edmonton, AB, Canada: Still Water Revival Books, 1991.

Gaebelein, Frank E., editor. *The Expositor's Bible Commentary Volume 2.* Grand Rapids, MI: Zondervan Publishing House, 1990.

————. *The Expositor's Bible Commentary Volume 8.* Grand Rapids, MI: Zondervan Publishing House, 1984.

Gaffin, Richard B. *Calvin and the Sabbath.* Scarsdale, NY: Westminster Discount Book Service, 1981.

Godet, Frederic Louis. *Commentary on Romans.* Grand Rapids, MI: Kregel Publications, 1979.

Griffiths, Michael. *Timothy and Titus.* Grand Rapids, MI: Baker Books, 1996.

Haldane, Robert. *An Exposition of the Epistle to the Romans.* Mac Dill AFB, Florida: Mac Donald Publishing Company, nd.

Harris, R. Laird, Gleason L. Archer, and Bruce K. Waltke. *Theological Wordbook of the Old Testament Volume I.* Chicago, IL: Moody Press, 1980.

Hendriksen, William. *New Testament Commentary, Thessalonians, Timothy and Titus.* Grand Rapids, MI: Baker Book House, re. 1981.

Hesselink, I. John. *Calvin's Concept of the Law.* Allison Park, PA: Pickwick Publications, 1992.

Hoch, Carl B., Jr. *All Things New.* Grand Rapids, MI: Baker Books, 1995.

Hughes, Philip Edgcumbe. *Paul's Second Epistle to the Corinthians.* Grand Rapids, MI: Wm. B. Eerdmans Publishing Co., 1962, re. 1986.

Kaiser, Walter C., Jr. *Toward an Old Testament Theology.* Grand Rapids, MI: Zondervan Publishing House, 1991.

————. *Toward Old Testament Ethics.* Grand Rapids, MI: Zondervan Publishing House, 1991.

Kent, Homer A., Jr. *The Pastoral Epistles.* Chicago, IL: Moody Press, 1986.

Keown, Gerald L., Pamela J. Scalise, and Thomas G. Smothers. *Word Biblical Commentary, Volume 27, Jeremiah 26–52.* Dallas, TX: Word Books, Publisher, 1995.

Knight, George W., III. *The Pastoral Epistles: A Commentary on the Greek Text.* Grand Rapids, MI: Wm. B. Eerdmans Company, 1992, re. 1996.

Kruse, Colin. *The Second epistle of Paul to the Corinthians.* Grand Rapids, MI: Wm. B. Eerdmans Company, 1987, re. 1997.

Lincoln, Andrew T. *Word Biblical Commentary: Ephesians.* Dallas, TX: Word Books, Publisher, 1990.

Lock, Walter. *A Critical and Exegetical Commentary on the Pastoral Epistles, (ICC).* Edinburgh, Scotland: T. & T. Clark, 1924, re. 1973.

MacArthur, John. *The MacArthur Study Bible.* Nashville, TN: Word Publishing, 1997.

McKane, William. *A Critical and Exegetical Commentary on Jeremiah Volume II.* Edinburgh, Scotland: T&T Clark, 1996.

Moo, Douglas. *The Epistle to the Romans.* Grand Rapids, MI: Wm. B. Eerdmans, Publishing Company, 1996.

Morris, William, editor. *The American Heritage Dictionary of the English Language*. New York, NY: American Heritage Publishing Co., Inc., 1969.

Moule, Handley C.G. *The Epistle to the Romans*. London, England: Pickering & Inglis Ltd., nd.

Murray, John. *The Epistle to the Romans*. Grand Rapids, MI: Wm. B. Eerdmans Publishing Co., 1984.

Nicoll, W. Robertson, editor. *The Expositor's Greek Testament Volume IV*. Grand Rapids, MI: Wm. B. Eerdmans Company, re. 1988.

Plummer, Alfred. *Cambridge Greek Testament for Schools and Colleges: The Second Epistle of Paul the Apostle to the Corinthians*. London, England: Cambridge University Press, 1912.

————. *The Pastoral Epistles*. New York, NY: Hodder & Stoughton, nd.

Poythress, Vern S. *The Shadow of Christ in the Law of Moses*. Phillipsburg, NJ: P&R Publishing, 1991.

Reisinger, Ernest C. *The Law and the Gospel*. Phillipsburg, NJ: P&R Publishing, 1997.

Reisinger, John G. *But I Say Unto You*. Southbridge, MA: Crown Publications, Inc., 1989.

————. *Christ, Lord and Lawgiver Over the Church*. Frederick, MD: New Covenant Media, 1998.

————. *John Bunyan on the Sabbath*. Webster, NY: Sound of Grace, nd.

————. *Tablets of Stone*. Southbridge, MA: Crown Publications, Inc., 1989.

Robertson, A.T. *A Grammar of the Greek New Testament in the Light of Historical Research*. Nashville, TN: Broadman Press, 1934.

Robertson, O. Palmer. *The Christ of the Covenants*. Phillipsburg, NJ: Presbyterian and Reformed Publishing Company, 1985.

Rogers, Cleon L., Jr., and Cleon L. Rogers, III. *The New Linguistic and Exegetical Key to the Greek New Testament*. Grand Rapids, MI: Zondervan Publishing House, 1998.

Sproul, R.C. *Ephesians*. Fearn Ross-shire, Scotland: Christian Focus Publications, 1994.

Stott, John. *Guard the Truth*. Downers Grove, IL: InterVarsity Press, 1996.

The Baptist Confession of Faith of 1689.

The Holy Bible containing the Old and New Testaments, The New King James Version. Nashville, TN: Nelson Publishers, 1984.

Turretin, Francis. *Institutes of Elenctic Theology Volume Two.* Phillipsburg, NJ: P&R Publishing, 1994.

Van Gemeren, Willem, General Editor. *New International Dictionary of Old Testament Theology and Exegesis Volume 2.* Grand Rapids, MI: Zondervan Publishing House, 1997.

Waldron, Samuel E. *Lectures on the Lord's Day.* Grand Rapids, MI: Truth for Eternity Ministries, nd.

Warfield, Benjamin B. *Selected Shorter Writings of Benjamin B. Warfield.* Phillipsburg, NJ: Presbyterian and Reformed Publishing Company, 1970.

Wendel, Francois. *Calvin, Origins and Developments of His Religious Thought.* Grand Rapids, MI: Baker Book House, 1997.

Wilson, Geoffrey B. *2 Corinthians, a Digest of Reformed Comment.* Carlisle, PA: The Banner of Truth Trust, 1979.

———. *The Pastoral Epistles.* Carlisle, PA: The Banner of Truth Trust, 1982.

To order more copies of

IN DEFENSE OF
THE DECALOGUE

call
Founders Ministries
at
(941) 772-1400